SCHOLASTIC

Handwriting
Jumbo Workbook

This book belongs to:

_____

Editor: Ourania Papacharalambous
Cover design: Tannaz Fassihi
Cover art: Gabriele Antonini
Interior design: Cynthia Ng
Interior illustrations: Joke and Fun Fact pages: Doug Jones
All other images: Shutterstock.com

ISBN 978-1-338-88755-6

Dear Family,

Welcome to *Handwriting Jumbo Workbook*! Clear handwriting is one of the best tools available to kids for expressing big ideas and showing what they know. Yet as young children head off to school, handwriting is often ignored. In the hustle and bustle of a hectic learning schedule—reading, writing, math, science, and social studies—few students have the time or inclination to perfect the fine art of crossing *t*'s and dotting *i*'s.

This workbook is the perfect tool to help children master the art of handwriting and continue their learning journey. The lively and funny handwriting practice pages will give handwriting the attention it deserves!

With just 5-10 minutes of practice each day, your child can spruce up his or her handwriting. How? The simple act of practicing letters or rewriting a sentence, fact, joke, or riddle motivates children to master the shape, size, and spacing of model script.

Read on to discover tips for using this resource to improve your child's handwriting and, in the process, his or her essential communication skills.

Sincerely,

The Editors

About This Book

Despite the use of electronic modes of communication, handwriting remains a part of our daily lives, whether it's jotting down a grocery list, writing a note or birthday card, filling out a form, brainstorming sessions, and more! There are even more benefits—it gives children (and adults) time to process what they are writing, which results in better retention of information.

The *Handwriting Jumbo Workbook* is here to provide practice with letter formation to strengthen children's writing skills. The activity pages are designed to engage children in:

- strengthening fine-motor skills
- recognizing letter shapes
- practicing the formation of each letter
- differentiating between letters that are often confused

Extra, Extra!

But wait, there's more! These special components are guaranteed to make learning extra fun...

WRITING ACTIVITIES

Throughout, children will also put their new handwriting skills to the test. They will practice writing letters, notes, lists, and more, nurturing their natural interest and helping them grow as writers.

MOTIVATING STICKERS

What better way to mark the milestones of your child's learning than with colorful stickers? After a workbook session, they're the perfect way to say: "Job well done!"

REWARD CERTIFICATE

Last, but not least, celebrate your child's handwriting success with this bright, pull-out certificate (page 320).

ONLINE LEARNING GAMES

Take learning online with fun learning games:
www.scholastic.com/success

Table of Contents

Handwriting Skills

Children progress through many stages on their way to conventional writing. Young children are writers long before they can use a pencil or crayon to form recognizable letters. The scribbles they draw in the sand or even in their food are the building blocks for letters that will lead to words.

As children's little hands gain more control of writing tools, their scribbles progress into circles, lines, and other more controlled shapes. Some of a child's early "writing" will become recognizable to him or her as the shapes that make up letters. As children begin to approach these lines and shapes with more confidence, their ability to write recognizable letters, such as those in their names, is not far off.

Handwriting practice reinforces recognition of the various features of letters and helps children see how letter shapes are connected. For example, *l* and *i* are made with vertical lines, *a* and *o* are made with circles, *t* and *f* have horizontal lines. As children become more familiar with the shapes of letters, their confidence in writing grows and they begin to make connections between letters and the sounds they represent. When children can make connections between letters, sounds, and the words they make, both their writing and reading skills grow.

Tips for Success

★ Although the activity pages are presented in a specific order, they can be completed in any order. You might suggest to your child that he or she begin by warming up with tracing lines and shapes, then to writing target letters, then to completing the jokes and facts and writing activities. However, if your child wants to start out of order, that's fine, too.

★ If you notice an error, gently model standard letter formation. This will help children rewire their handwriting habits, which will improve both the clarity and speed of their printing down the road.

★ Pick a good time for your child to work on the worksheets. You should always choose a time when your child is not too tired.

★ Make sure your child has all the supplies he or she needs, such as pencils and an eraser. Designate a special place for your child to work.

★ Encourage your child to complete the worksheets, but don't force the issue. It is important that he or she maintains a positive and relaxed attitude.

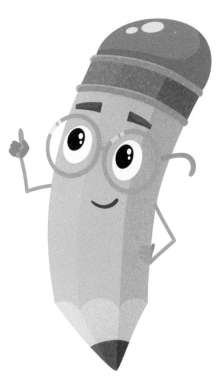

★ When your child has finished the workbook, present him or her with the certificate at the end of the book. Feel free to frame or laminate the certificate and display it for everyone to see. Your child will be so proud!

FINE-MOTOR SKILLS

Remember, each child progresses at a different rate. To help your child develop and improve his or her fine-motor skills, have crayons and washable markers accessible. Encourage your child to trace, doodle, and draw. Then, proudly display your child's creations on a festive bulletin board or your refrigerator.

SUPPLIES: crayons or washable markers

These fish can fly! Color the wings.

The leopard has lost its spots. Draw spots on the leopard.

The octopus is missing five arms. Draw them.

Color the picture. Use the Color Key. What did you make?

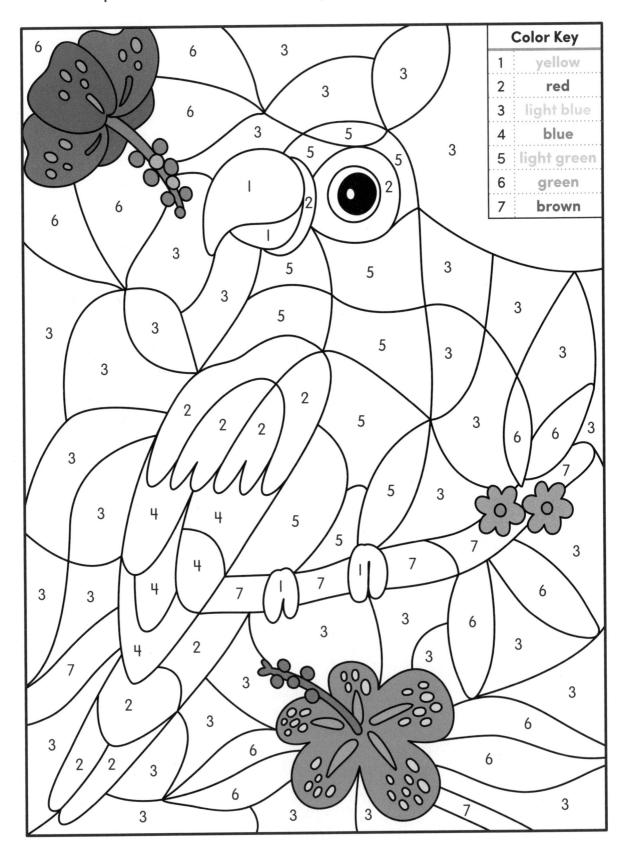

Color Key

1	yellow
2	red
3	light blue
4	blue
5	light green
6	green
7	brown

© Scholastic Inc.

Trace the petals on the flowers.
Then, color each flower.

This quilt is unfinished! Add lines, circles, squiggles, and color to finish the quilt.

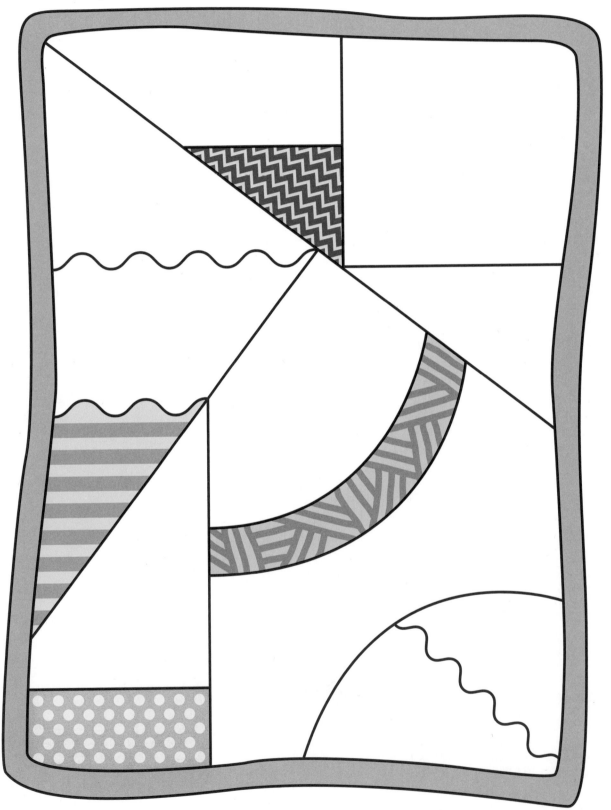

Design your own hot-air balloon. Quick, it's already in the air!

Design your own matching t-shirt and shorts set.

GET READY TO WRITE

This section provides details about the correct position for left-handed and right-handed writers, the types of lines letters make, and practice with those lines. Children also trace straight lines, wavy lines, connecting lines, and more.

To reinforce learning, use a pencil to draw simple dashed-line drawings on paper. Then, challenge your child to trace over them with crayons or markers.

SUPPLIES: crayons, washable markers, pencils

Left-Handed Writing

Place the left corner of the paper you are writing on higher.

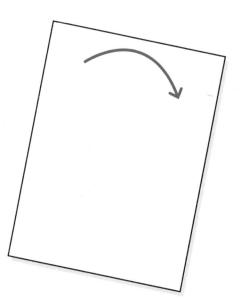

Hold your pencil in your left hand between your thumb and your first finger. You can also hold the pencil between your thumb and your first two fingers. The top of the pencil should point toward your left shoulder.

Lean slightly forward.

Set your feet flat on the floor.

© Scholastic Inc.

Right-Handed Writing

Place the right corner of the paper you are writing on higher.

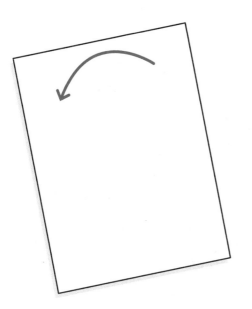

Hold your pencil in your right hand between your thumb and your first finger. You can also hold the pencil between your thumb and your first two fingers. The top of the pencil should point toward your right shoulder.

Lean slightly forward.

Set your feet flat on the floor.

Up and Down

Tip: Some letters and numbers have lines that are straight. They go top to bottom or bottom to top.

Trace the lines from top to bottom.

Trace the lines from bottom to top.

Trace the line in each letter and number that is straight up and down.

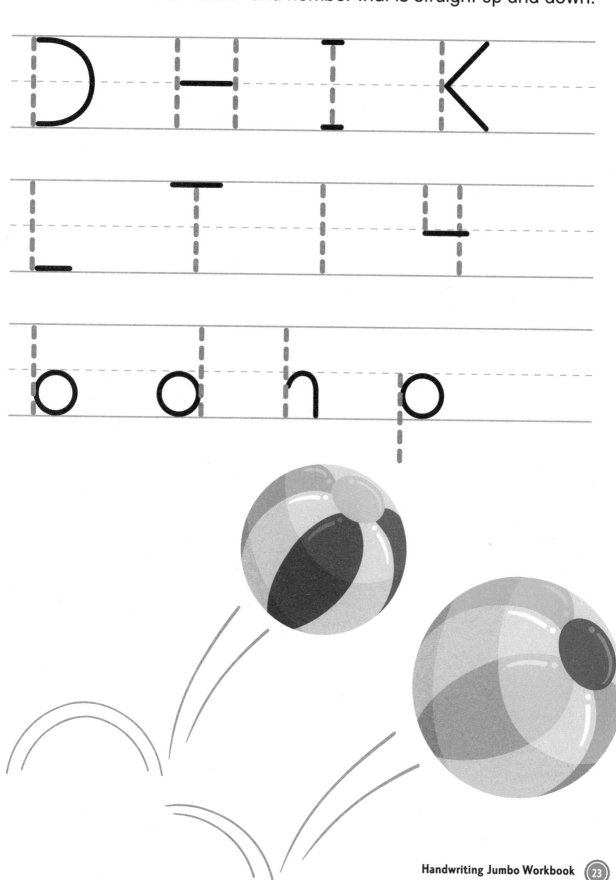

Side to Side

Trace the lines from left to right.

Trace the lines from right to left.

© Scholastic Inc.

Trace the line in each letter and number that goes side to side.

E F G T

z f 5 7

t L e 4

Around in Circles

Trace the forward circles.

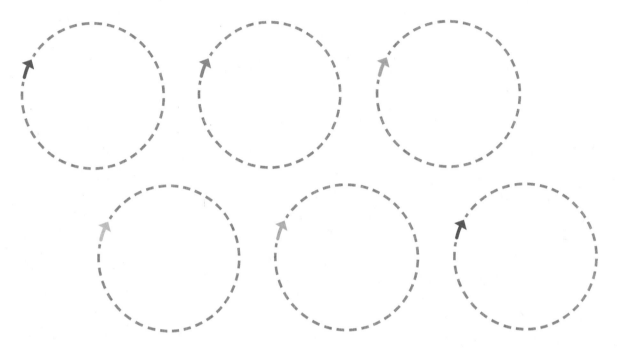

Trace the backward circles.

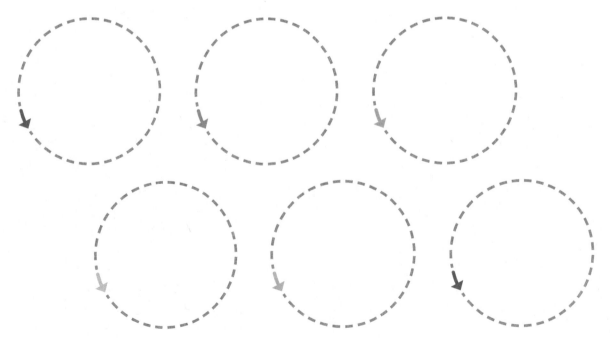

Trace the line in each letter and number that makes a circle.

B C D O

b e g q

3 6 8 9

Lean Left, Lean Right

Tip: Some letters and numbers have lines that slant right, others have lines that slant left.

Trace the lines that slant right.
Follow the arrows.

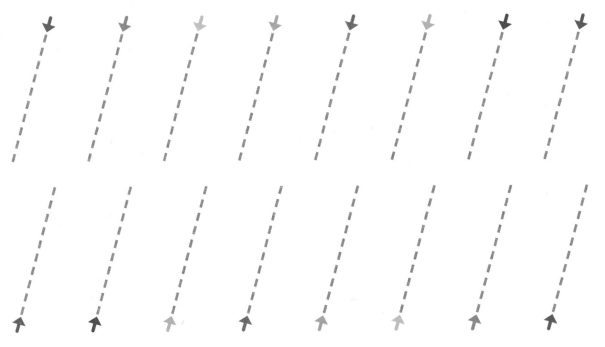

Trace the lines that slant left. Follow the arrows.

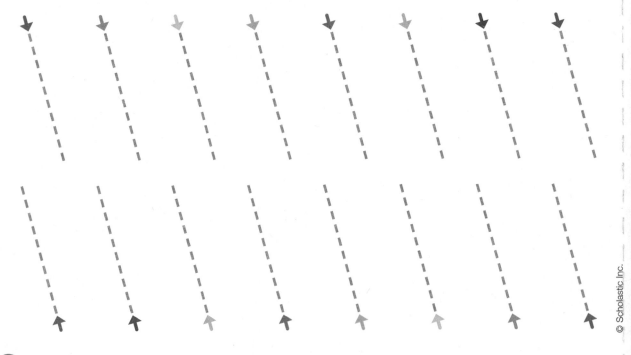

Trace the line in each letter and number that slants left or right.

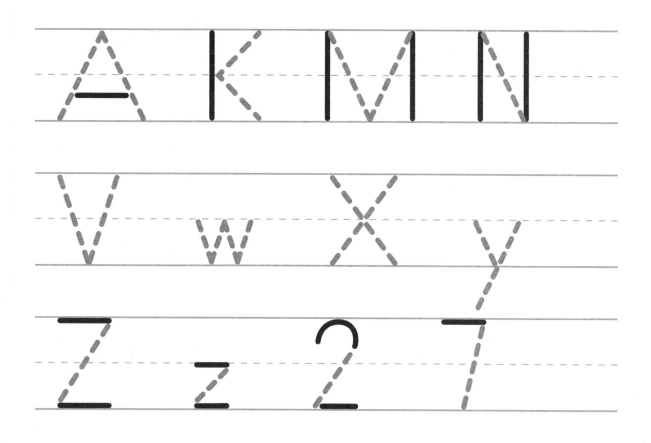

A K M N

V W X Y

Z z 2 7

Trace the lines.

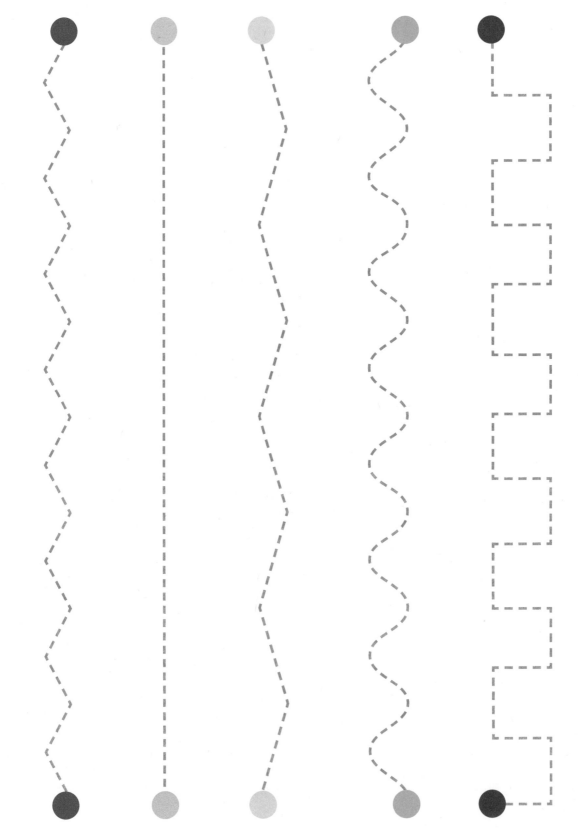

Trace the lines.

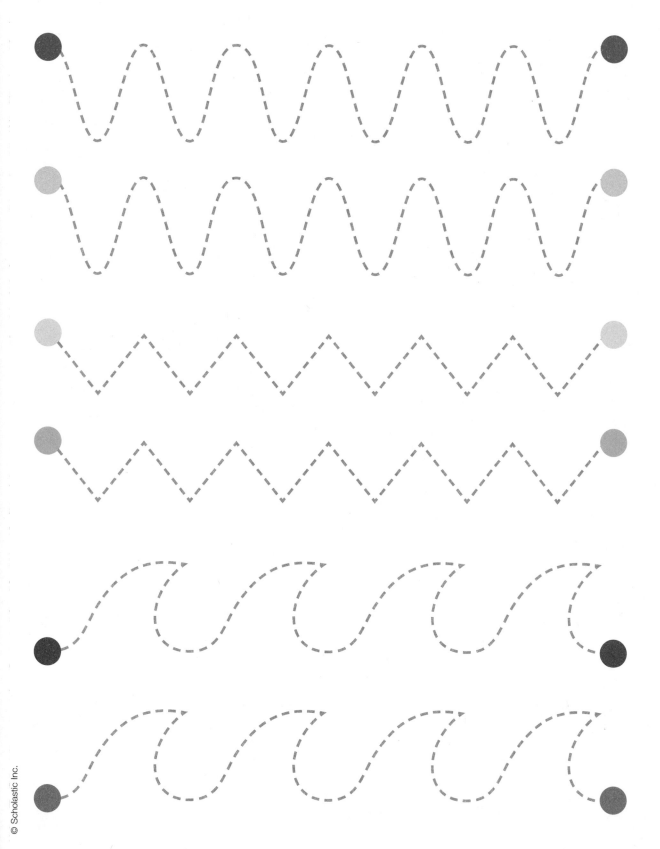

Trace the lines.

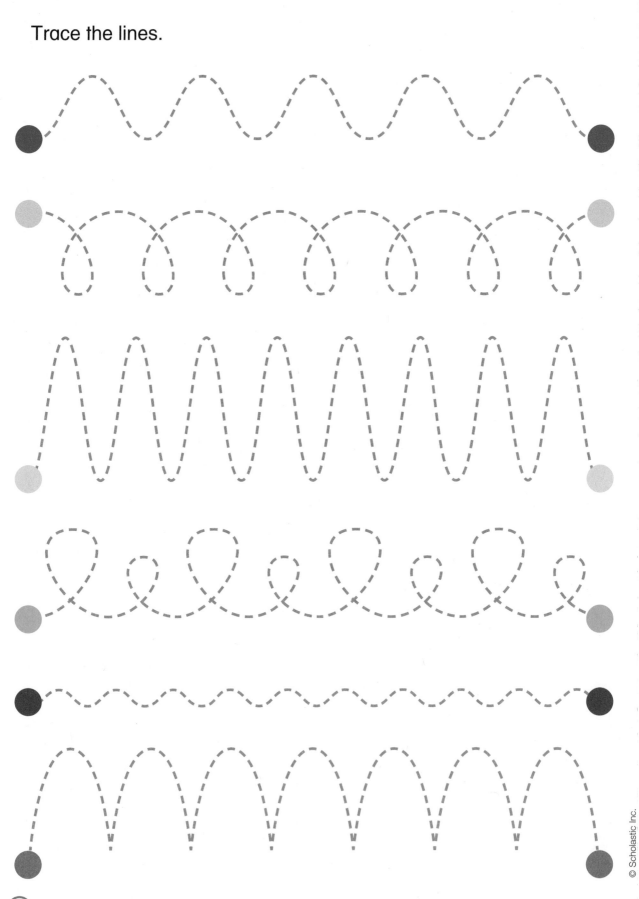

Trace each path.

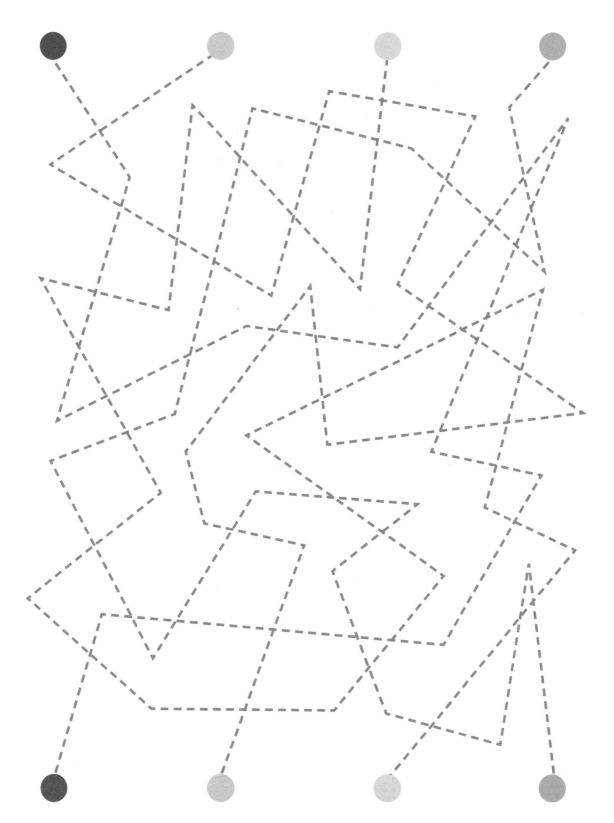

Trace each path.

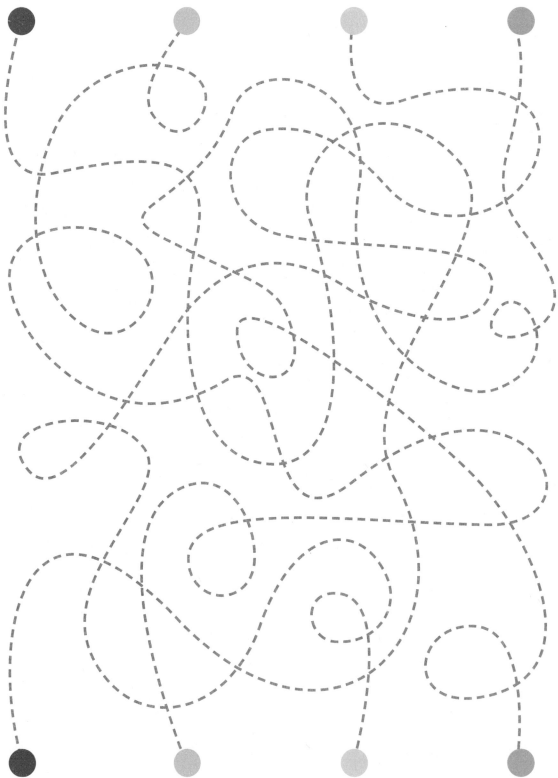

HANDWRITING

This section provides loads of practice writing the letters of the alphabet, simple sentences, numbers, and more.

Extend the writing activity by asking your child to draw a picture that illustrates the sentence. Then, have him or her write the sentence under the picture.

SUPPLIES: crayons, washable markers, pencils

Trace and write.

Trace and write.

Trace.

Aliyah

ants

Aliyah adores ants.

Bb

Trace and write.

B B B B B

Trace and write.

b b b b b

Trace.

Bert

bears

Bert barks at bears.

Trace each **A** and **a**. Then, follow each **A** and **a** to help the ant get to the apple.

Trace each **B** and **b**. Then, color the squares with **B** and **b**.

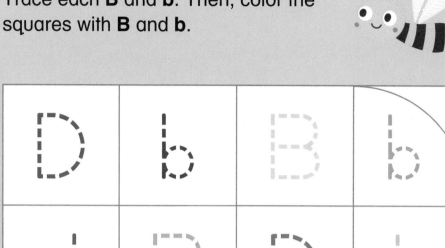

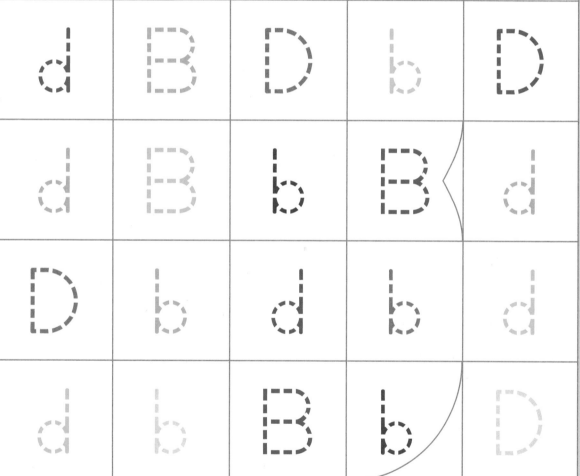

Cc

Trace and write.

C   C   C   C   C

Trace and write.

c   c   c   c   c

Trace.

Carl

cats

Carl cares for cats.

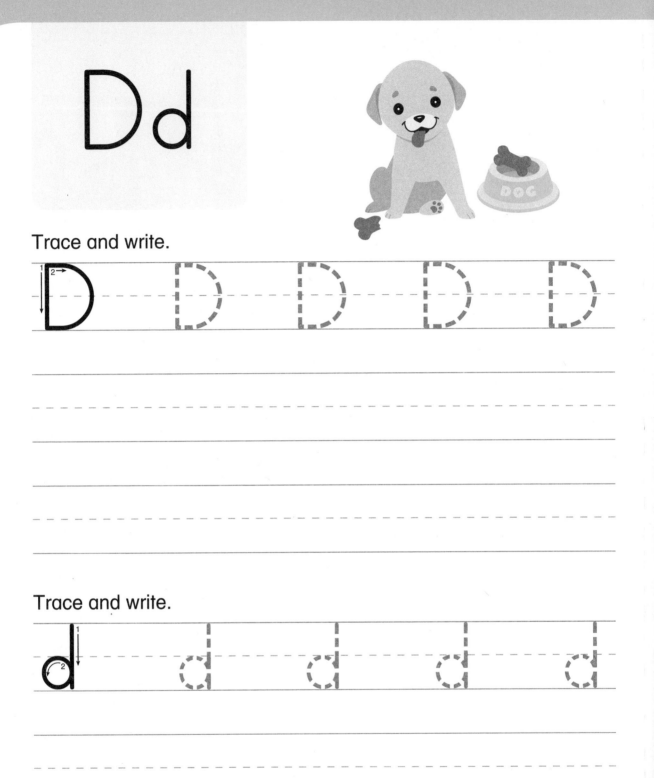

Trace and write.

Trace and write.

Trace.

Diego

dogs

Diego draws dogs.

Trace each **C** and **c**. Then, circle your favorite cupcake.

Trace each **D** and **d**. Then, color the spaces with **D** and **d**.

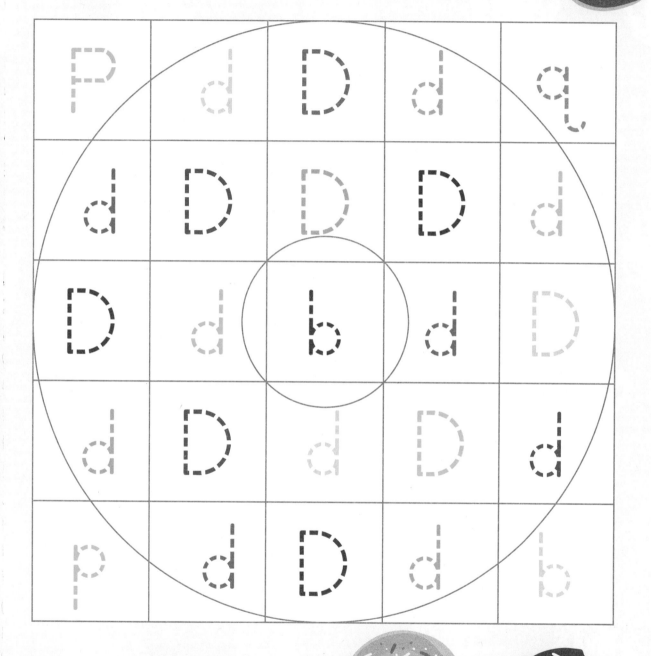

Ee

Trace and write.

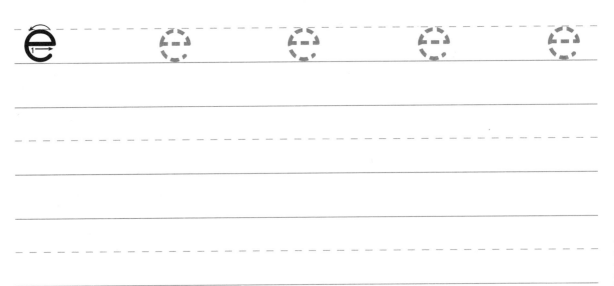

Trace and write.

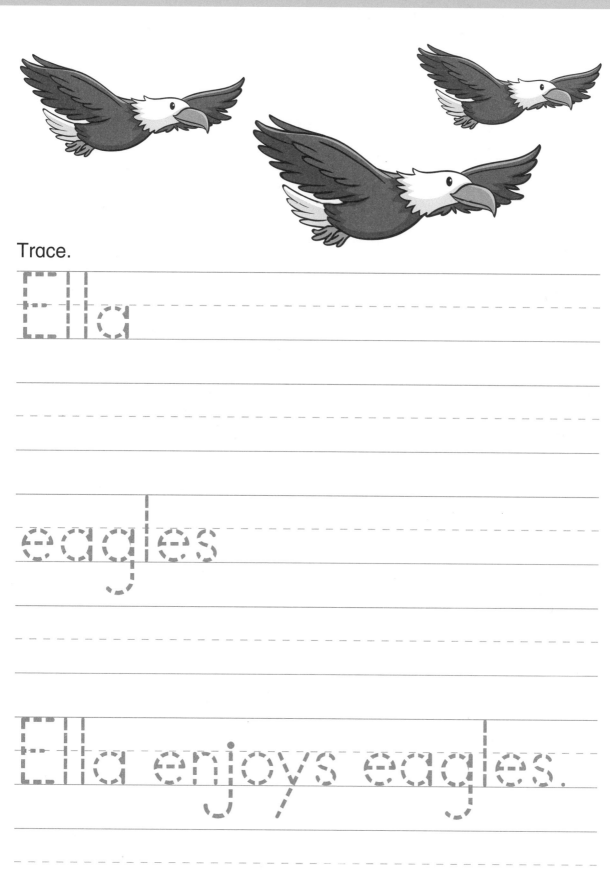

Trace.

Ella

eagles

Ella enjoys eagles.

F f

Trace and write.

Trace and write.

Trace.

Felix

frogs

Felix feeds frogs.

Trace each **E** and **e**. Then, follow each **E** and **e** to help the elephant get to the envelope.

START

L   a

E   T

c

e   E   f   c

E

e   F

e   t

E   E

I   L

a   FINISH

Trace each **F** and **f**. Then, color the squares with **F** and **f**.

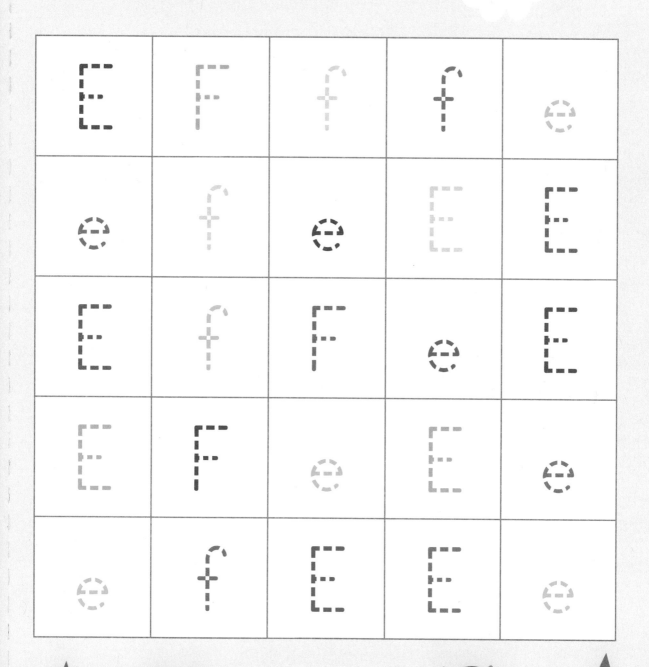

Gg

Trace and write.

G   G   G   G   G

Trace and write.

g   g   g   g   g

Trace.

Gail

goats

Gail grins at goats.

Hh

Trace and write.

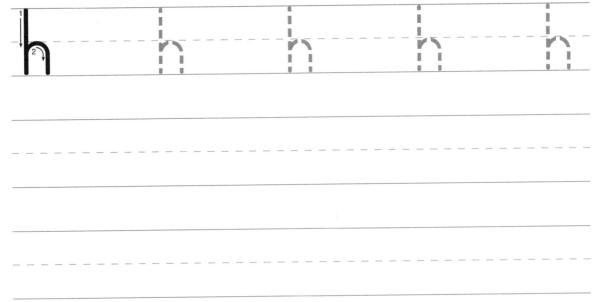

Trace and write.

Trace.

Harry

horse

Harry has a horse.

Trace each **G** and **g**. Then, circle your favorite guitar.

Trace each **H** and **h**. Then, color the spaces with **H** and **h**.

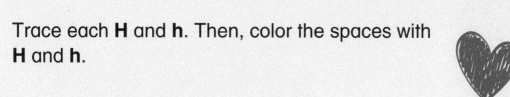

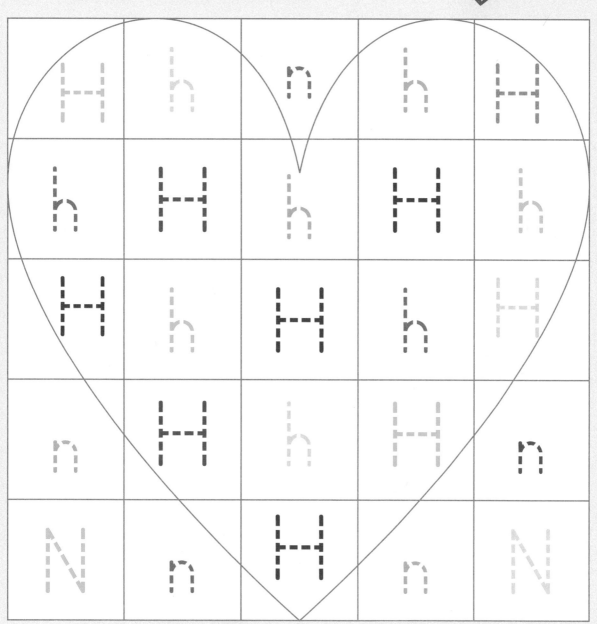

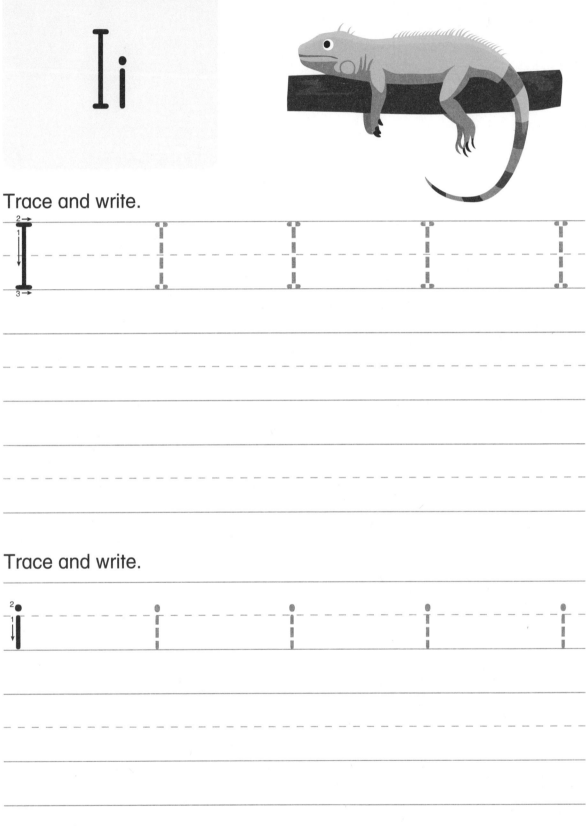

Trace and write.

Trace and write.

Trace.

Iris

iguana

Iris is an iguana.

Jj

Trace and write.

J

Trace and write.

j

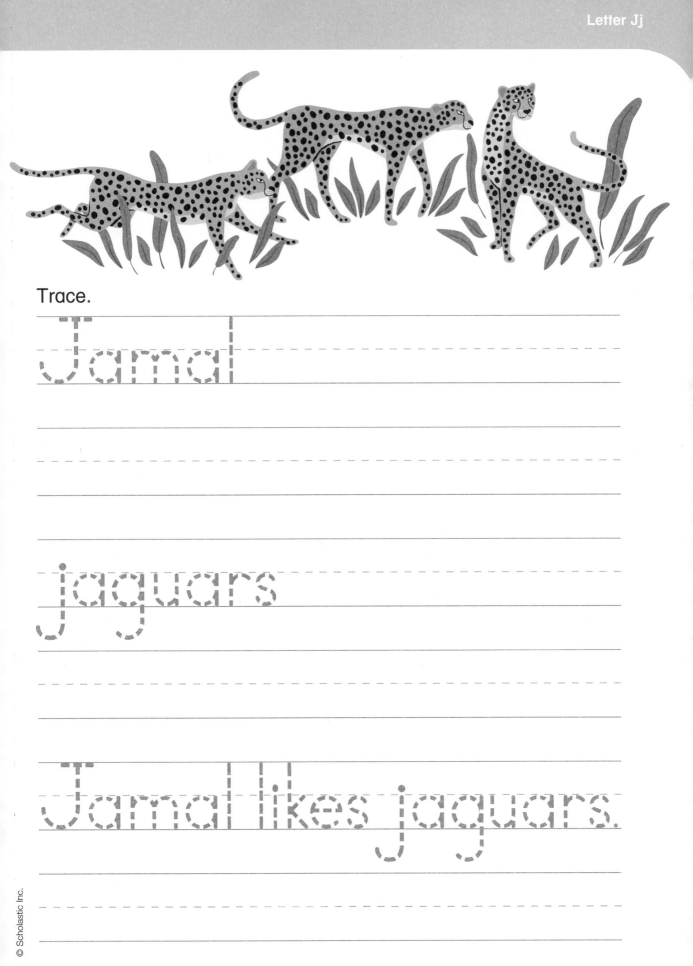

Trace.

Jamal

jaguars

Jamal likes jaguars.

Trace each **I** and **i**. Then, follow each
I and **i** to help the inchworm get to the invitation.

START

I   X

i   c

k   Y   e   I

K   i

V   I

v   c   i

X

I   i   I   k

i

I   i   I

i   FINISH

YOU'RE INVITED!

Trace each **J** and **j**. Then, color the squares with **J** and **j**.

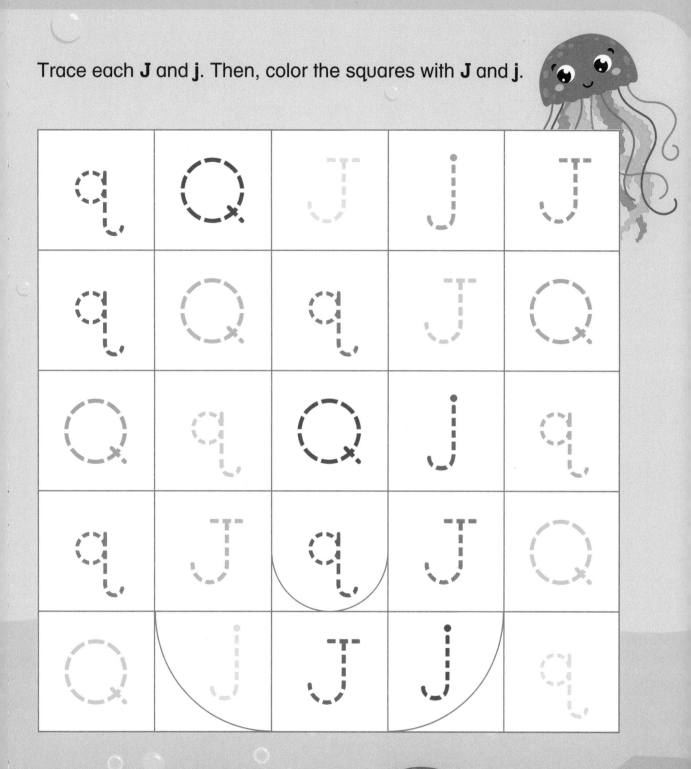

Kk

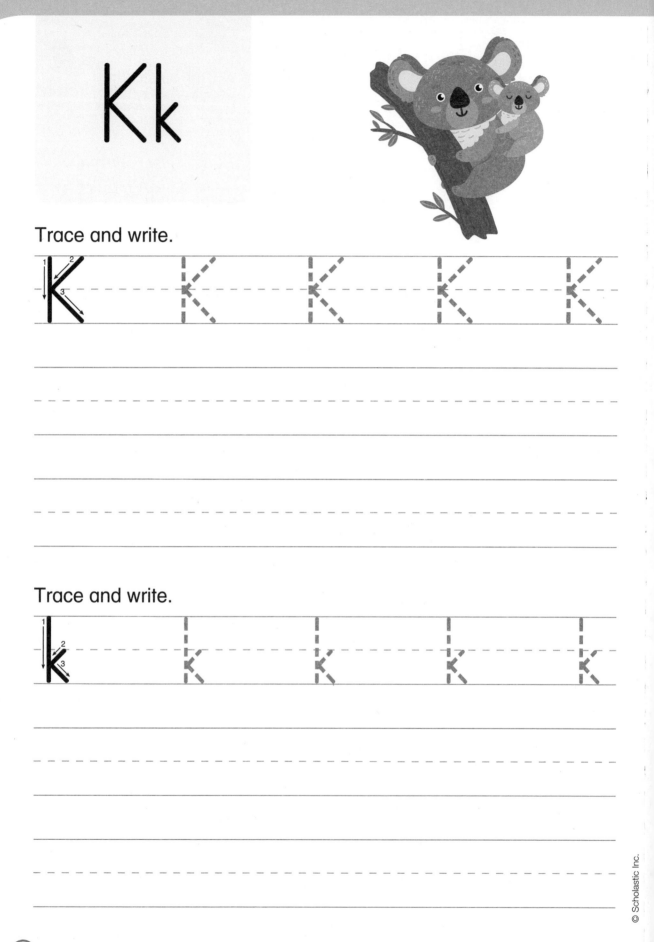

Trace and write.

Trace and write.

Trace.

Kiara

koala

Kiara is a koala.

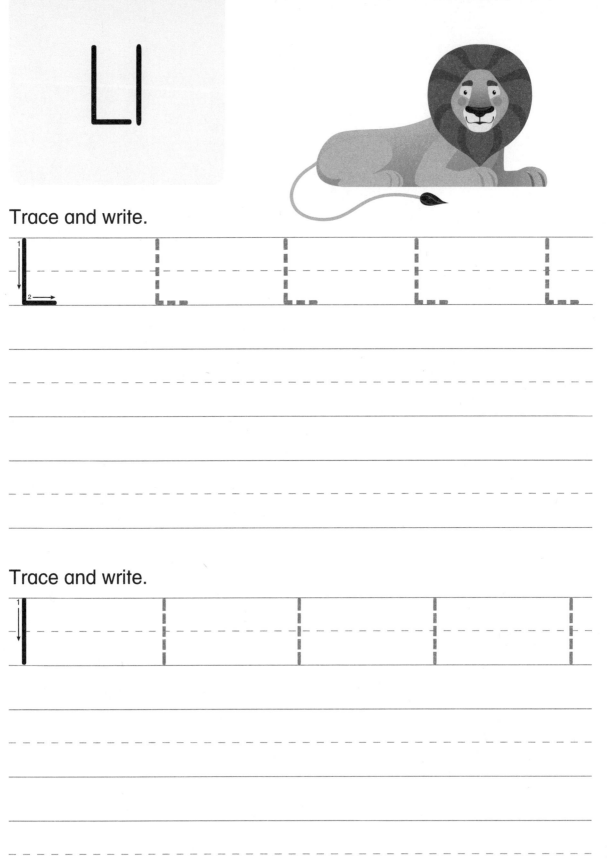

Trace and write.

Trace and write.

Trace.

Logan

lions

Logan likes lions.

Trace each **K** and **k**. Then, circle your favorite kite.

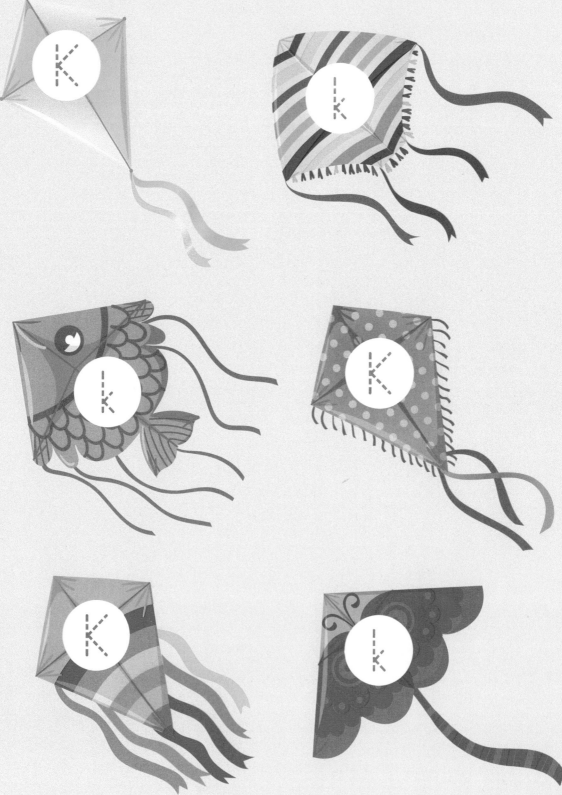

Trace each **L** and **I**. Then, color the spaces with **L** and **I**.

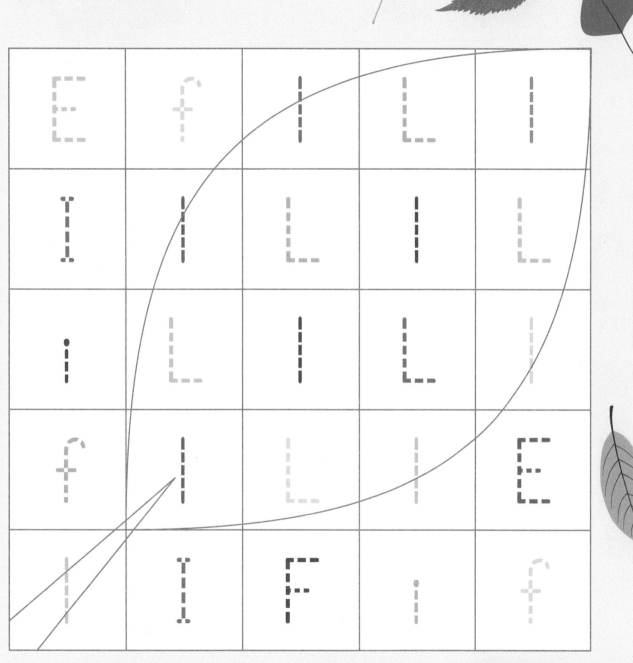

E	f	I	L	I
I	I	L	I	L
i	L	I	L	I
f	i	L	I	E
I	I	F	i	f

Mm

Trace and write.

M M M M M M M

Trace and write.

m m m m m

Trace.

Mia

monkey

Mia is a monkey.

Trace and write.

Trace and write.

Trace.

Neil

newts

Neil likes newts.

Trace each **M** and **m**. Then, follow each **M** and **m** to help the mouse get to the mountain.

START

FINISH

Trace each **N** and **n**. Then, color the squares with **N** and **n**.

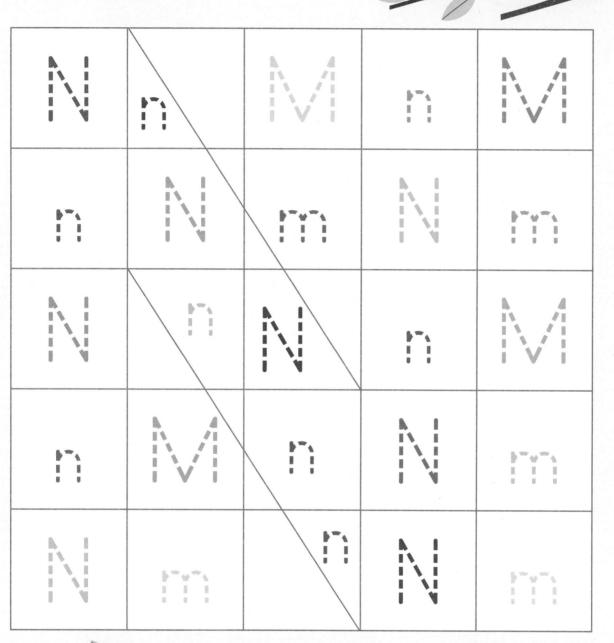

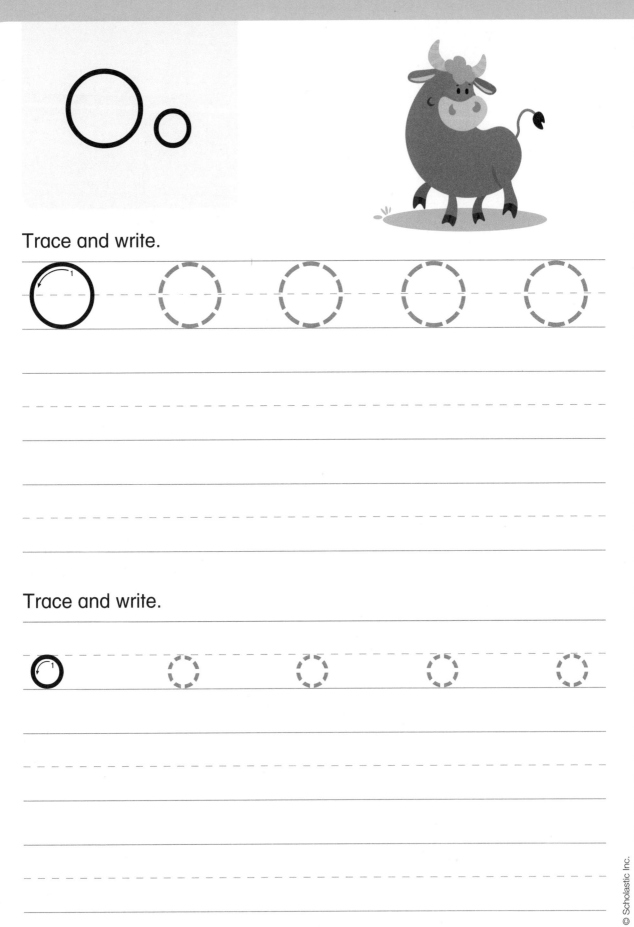

Trace and write.

Trace and write.

Trace.

Olga

oxen

Olga owns oxen.

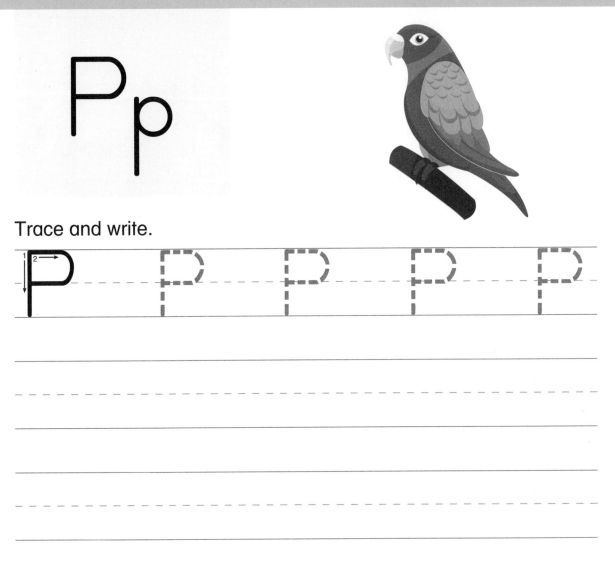

Trace and write.

Trace and write.

Trace.

Pablo

parrot

Pablo has a parrot.

Trace each **O** and **o**. Then, circle your favorite octopus.

Trace each **P** and **p**. Then, color the spaces with **P** and **p**.

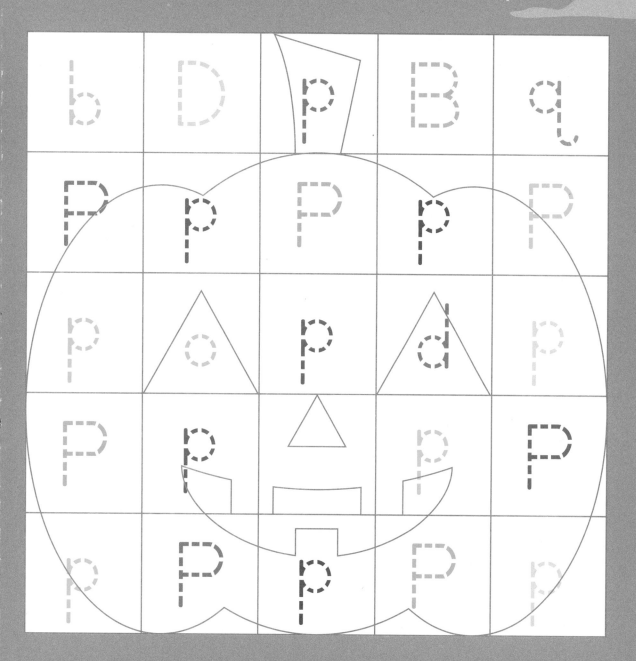

Qq

Trace and write.

Trace and write.

Trace.

Quisha

quail

Quisha is a quail.

Trace and write.

Trace and write.

Trace.

Raul

rabbits

Raul raises rabbits.

Trace each **Q** and **q**. Then, follow each **Q** and **q** to help the queen get to her quilt.

START

FINISH

© Scholastic Inc.

Trace each **R** and **r**. Then, color the squares with **R** and **r**.

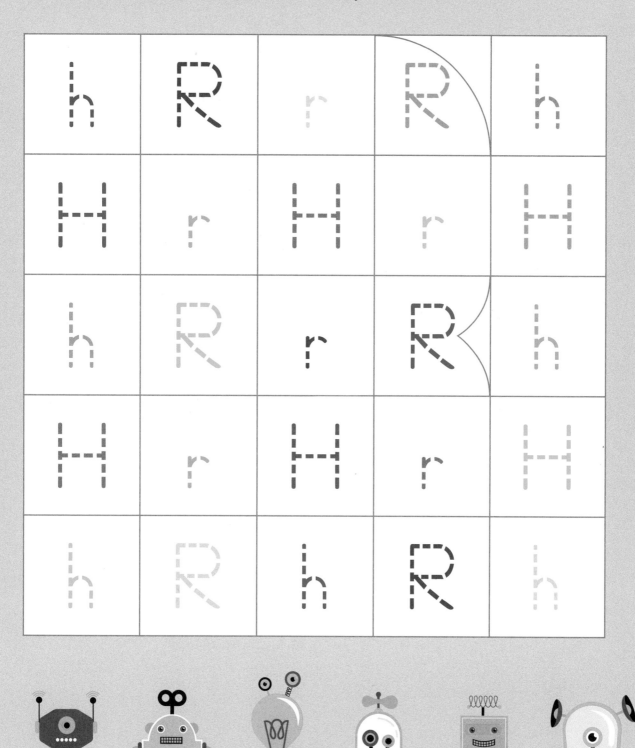

Ss

Trace and write.

S S S S S

Trace and write.

s s s s s

Trace.

Sasha

sheep

Sasha sees sheep.

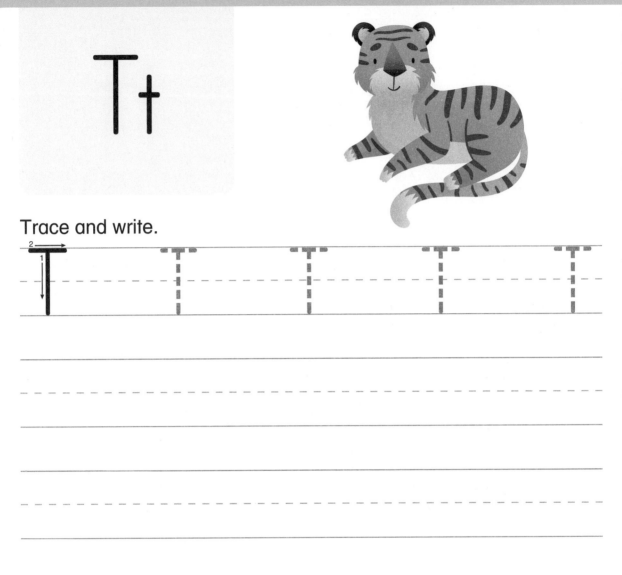

Trace and write.

Trace and write.

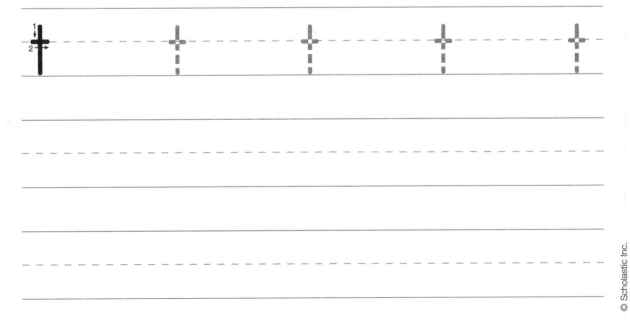

Trace.

Tom

tigers

Tom likes tigers.

Trace each **S** and **s**. Then, circle your favorite sweater.

Trace each **T** and **t**. Then, color the spaces with **T** and **t**.

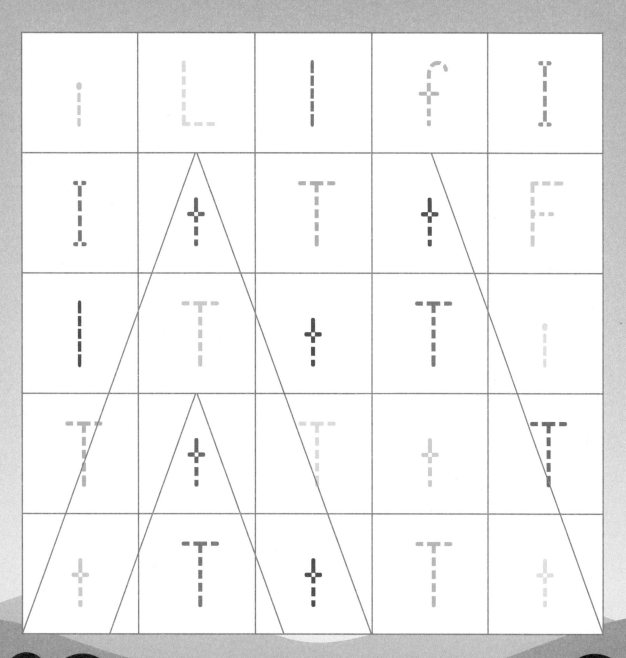

Uu

Trace and write.

U U U U U

Trace and write.

u u u u u

Trace.

Umi

unicorn

Umi likes unicorns.

V v

Trace and write.

V V V V V

Trace and write.

V V V V V

Trace.

Van

vulture

Van saw a vulture.

Trace each **U** and **u**. Then, follow each **U** and **u** to help the unicorn get to the umbrella.

START

FINISH

Trace each **V** and **v**. Then, color the squares with **V** and **v**.

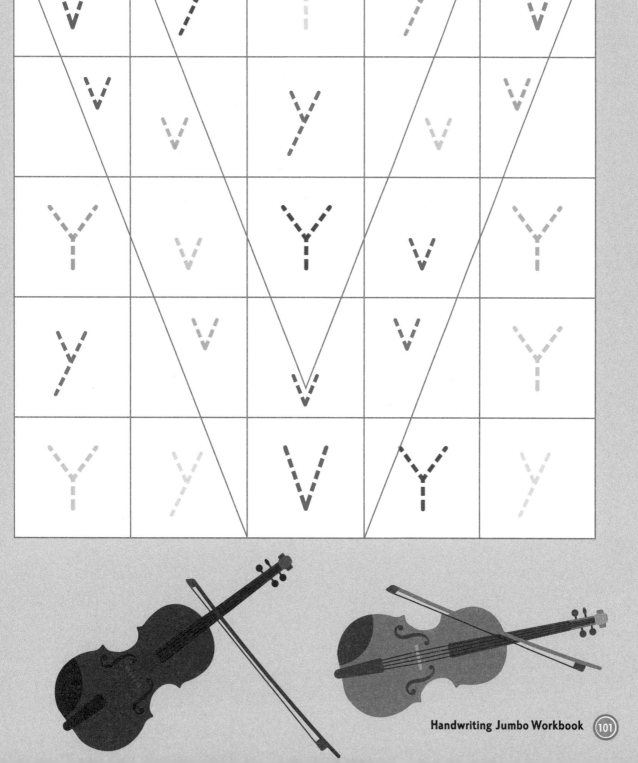

© Scholastic Inc.

Trace and write.

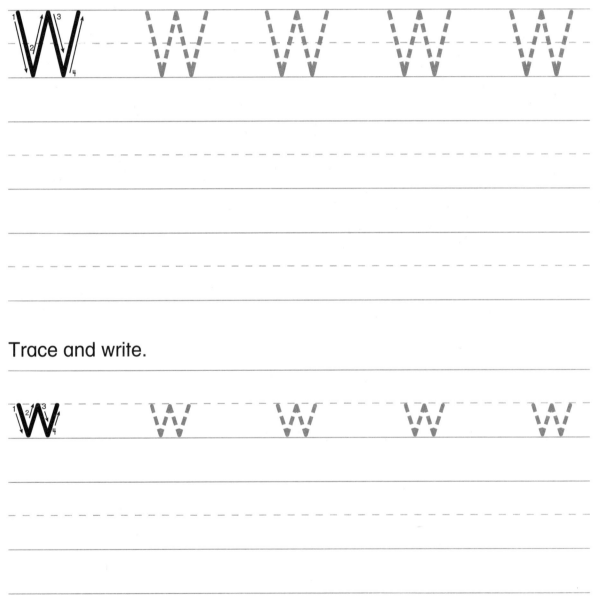

Trace and write.

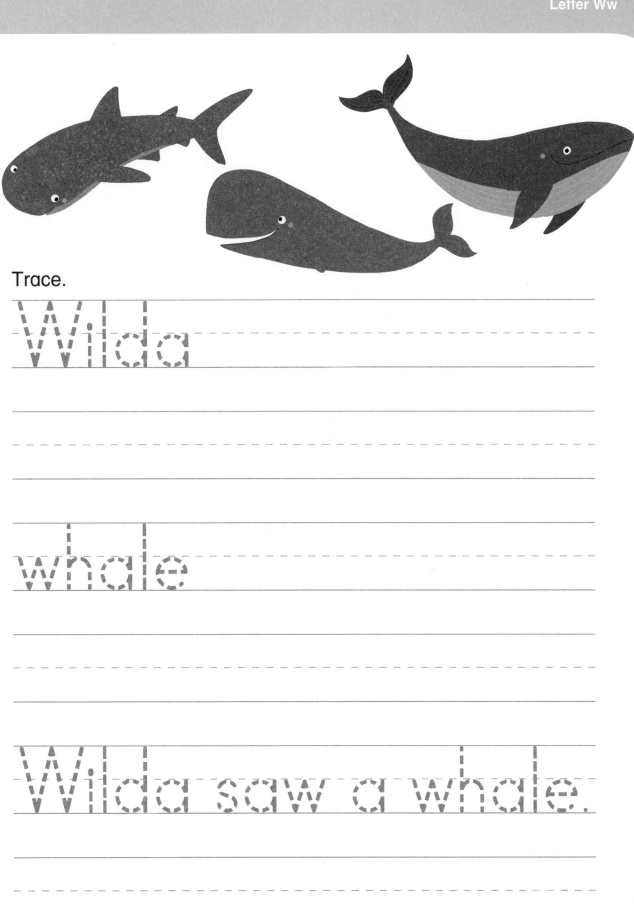

Trace.

Wilda

whale

Wilda saw a whale.

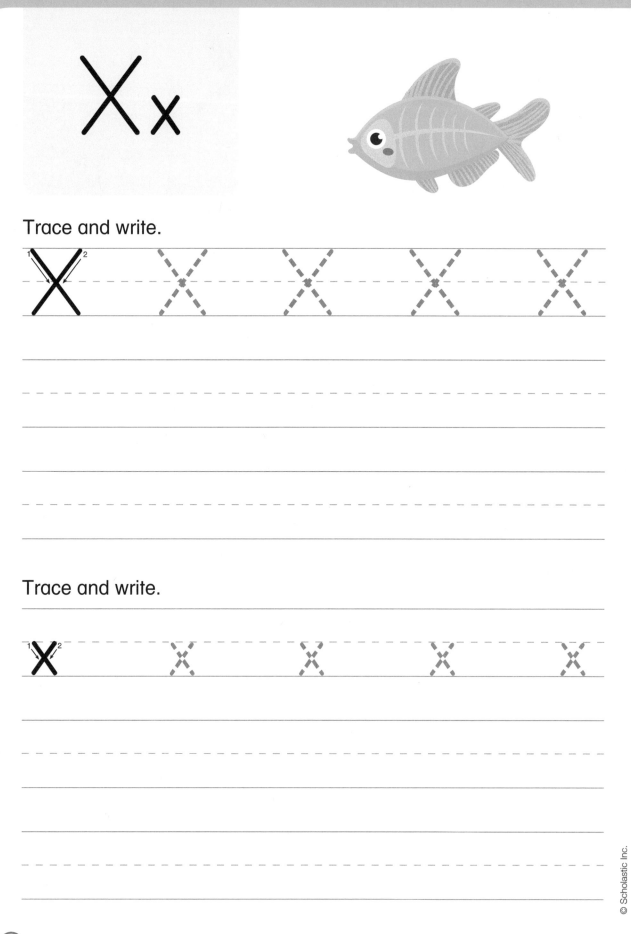

Trace and write.

Trace and write.

Trace.

Xen

x-ray fish

Xen is an x-ray fish.

Trace each **W** and **w**. Then, circle your favorite whale.

Trace each **X** and **x**. Then, color the squares with **X** and **x**.

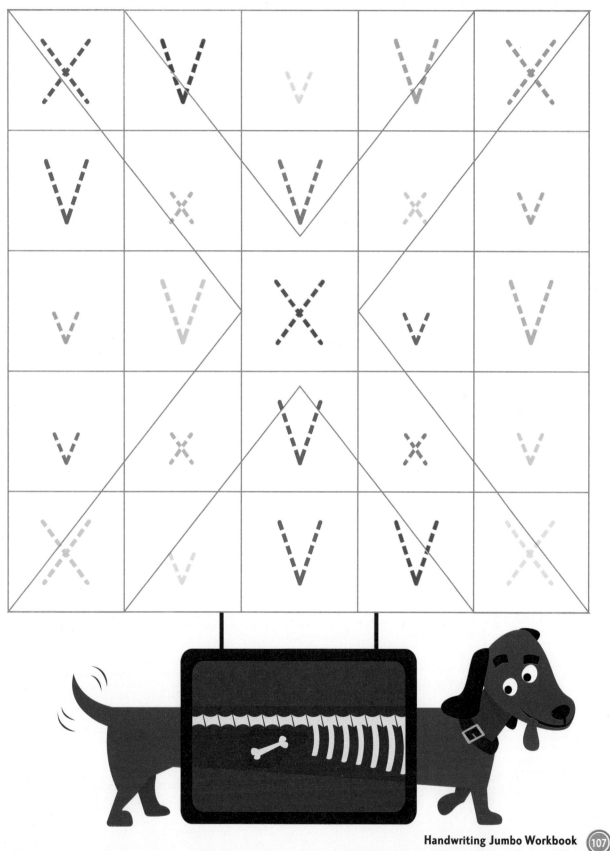

Trace and write.

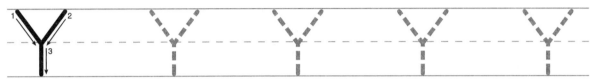

Trace and write.

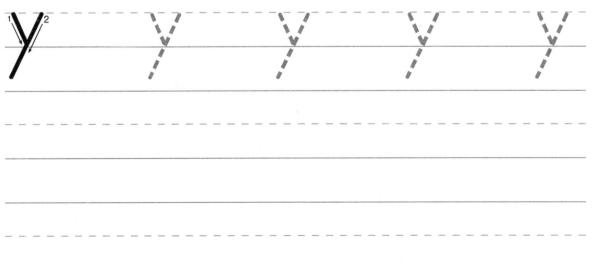

Trace.

Yara

yaks

Yara yaps at yaks.

Zz

Trace and write.

Trace and write.

Trace.

Zane

zebra

Zane is a zebra.

Trace each **Y** and **y**. Then, follow each **Y** and **y** to help the yak get to the yo-yo.

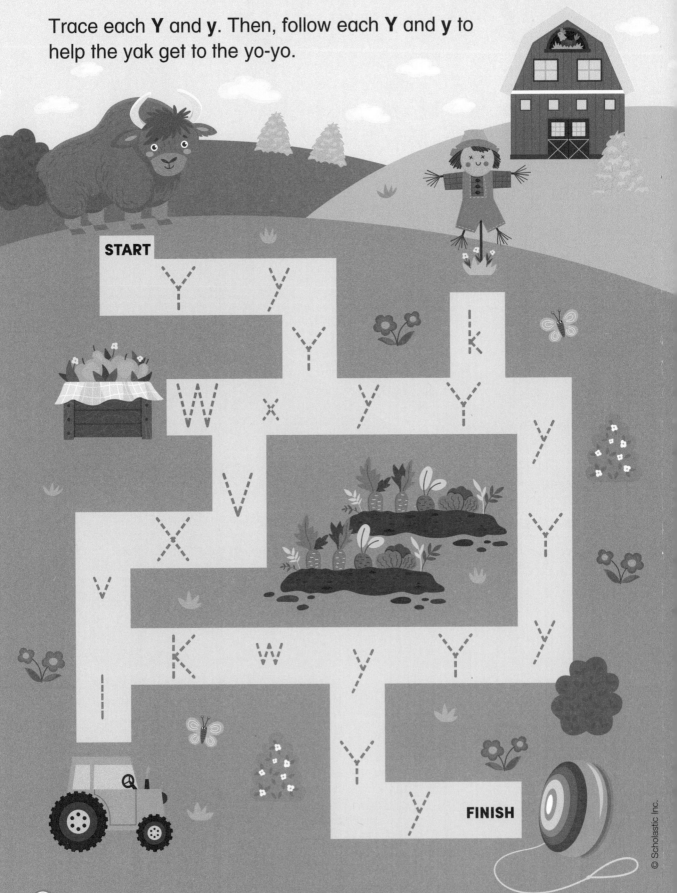

© Scholastic Inc.

Trace each **Z** and **z**. Then, color the spaces with **Z** and **z**.

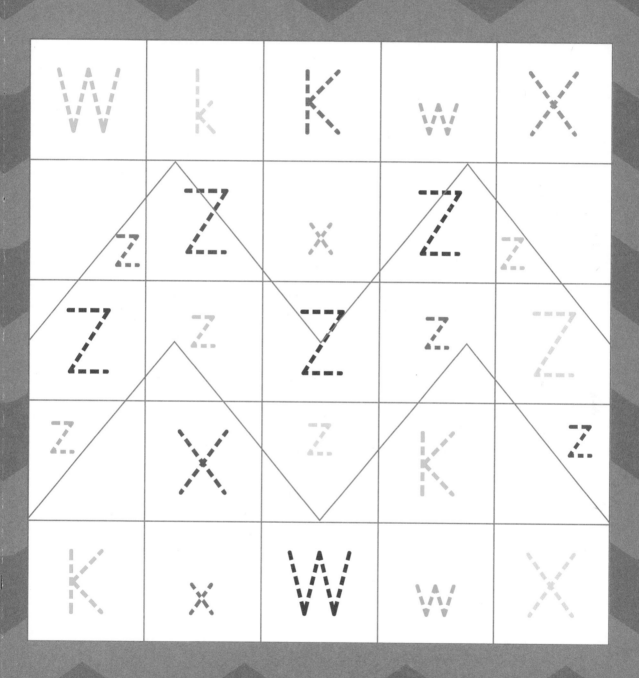

Trace and write.

© Scholastic Inc.

Trace and write.

one

two

four

three

five

Trace and write.

one

two

three

four

five

six

seven

eight

ten

nine

Trace and write.

six

seven

eight

nine

ten

Trace and write.

Monday

Tuesday

Wednesday

Thursday

Friday

Saturday

Sunday

JOKES, RIDDLES, FUN FACTS & MORE

This section is full of handwriting tips, jokes, riddles, fun facts, and writing activities. After your child has completed an activity ask him or her to read the joke, riddle, or fact to you. Proudly display writing activities for all to see.

SUPPLIES: pencils

Use your best handwriting to copy the words.

Tip:
Begin letters from the top, not the bottom.

dogs

cats

you

Bonus Chuckle!

Why do dogs always run in circles?
Because it's hard to run in squares!

Use your best handwriting to copy the sentence below.

Why should you stay inside when it is raining cats and dogs? Because you might step in a poodle!

Use your best handwriting to copy the words.

kind

sound

cats

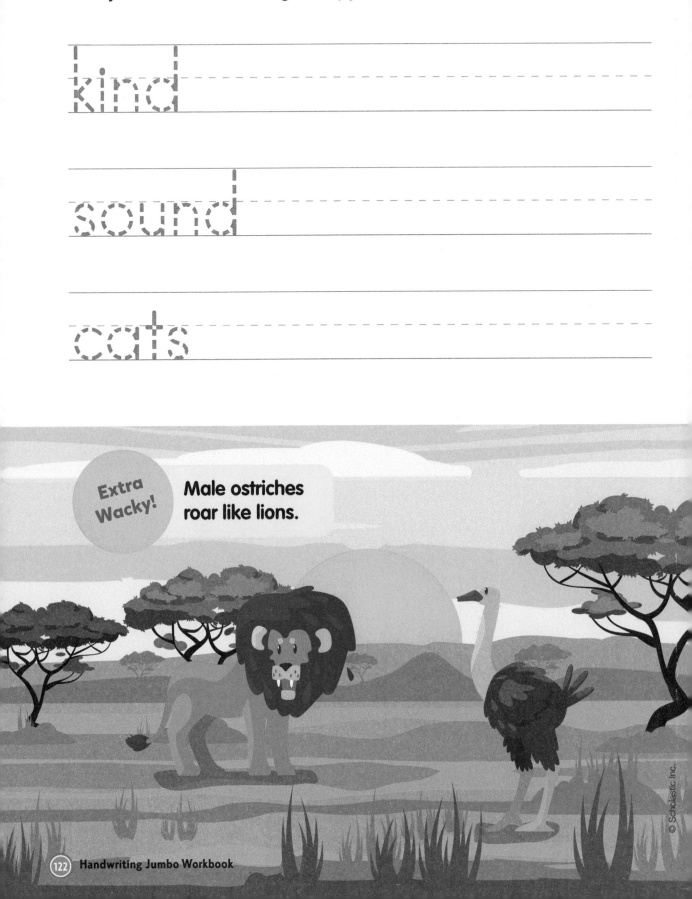

Extra Wacky! **Male ostriches roar like lions.**

Use your best handwriting to copy the sentence below.

Do you know what kind of sound cheetahs make? These fierce, fast cats chirp like little birds.

CHIRP!

CHIRP!

Use your best handwriting to copy the words.

of

kitten

glass

Bonus Chuckle!

What is a cat's favorite breakfast food?
Mice Crispies!

© Scholastic Inc.

Use your best handwriting to copy the sentence below.

What happened to the kitten that drank a big glass of lemonade? She became a real sourpuss!

Use your best handwriting to copy the words.

Do

play

sport

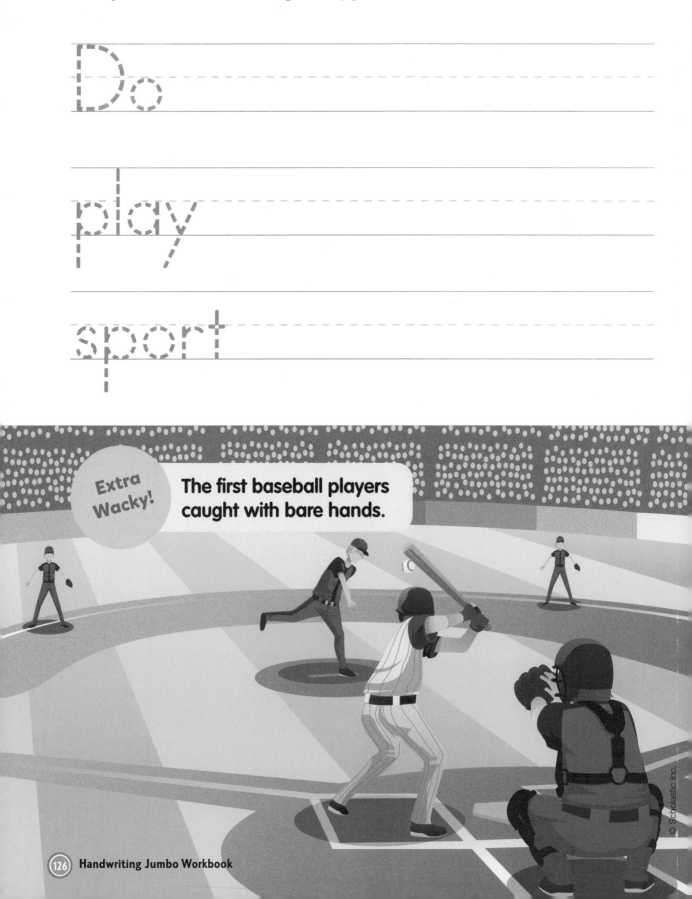

Extra Wacky! The first baseball players caught with bare hands.

Use your best handwriting to copy the sentence below.

Do you play soccer?
More than 240 million
people all around the
world play this very sport!

Trace and write.

cook

eat

walk

drink

read

sleep

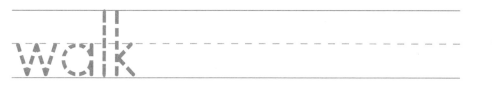

Choose an action word from page 128. Draw a picture of yourself doing that activity. Then, write about your picture.

Use your best handwriting to copy the words.

Tip:
Use your pinkie finger or a paper clip to measure the space between each word.

gray

and

slipper

Bonus Chuckle!

What is gray, has a wand, and gives money to elephants?
The tusk fairy!

Use your best handwriting to copy the sentence below.

What is gray, weighs five thousand pounds, and wears a dainty glass slipper? Cinderelephant!

Use your best handwriting to copy the words.

most

are

like

Extra Wacky!

It takes 50 licks to finish an ice cream cone.

Use your best handwriting to copy the sentence below.

Vanilla is the most popular ice cream flavor. But there are some other odd flavors to try, like popcorn and hot dog!

Use your best handwriting to copy the words.

Tip:
All uppercase letters should touch the top and the bottom lines.

climb

top

inside

Bonus Chuckle!

What happened when the gorilla ate too much candy?
He got a belly-ape!

Use your best handwriting to copy the sentence below.

Why did King Kong climb to the top of the Empire State Building? Because he could not fit inside the elevator!

Use your best handwriting to copy the words.

it

wonder

ride

Extra Wacky! **A mosquito can flap its wings 500 times a second!**

Use your best handwriting to copy the sentence below.

Ever wonder what mosquitoes do when it rains? Sometimes one lands on a drop of water and catches a ride!

WHEEEEEEE

Trace and write.

talk

dance

write

run

play

sing

Choose an action word from page 138. Draw a picture of yourself doing that activity. Then, write about your picture.

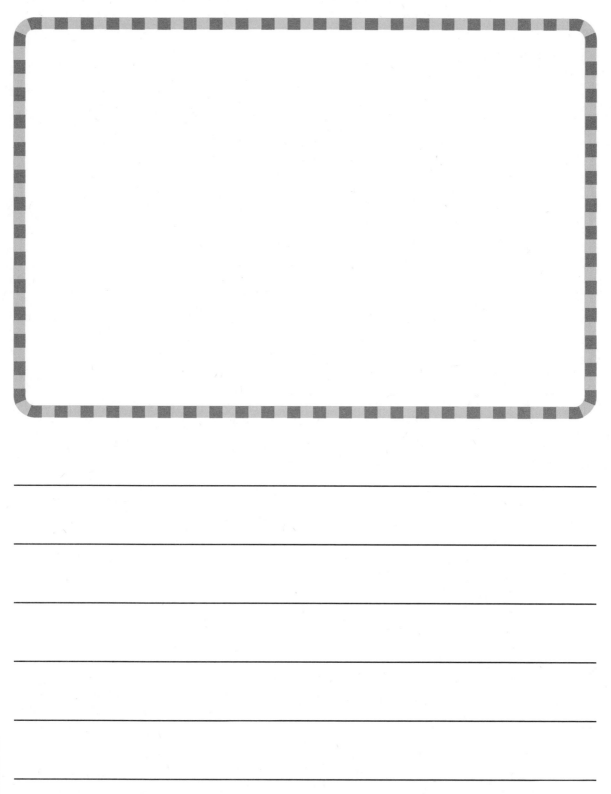

_____

_____

_____

_____

_____

Use your best handwriting to copy the words.

Tip:
Lowercase letters **b**, **d**, **f**, **h**, and **l** are tall. They all touch the top line.

fish

ocean

goes

Bonus Chuckle!

What is the best way to communicate with a fish?
Drop it a line!

© Scholastic Inc.

Use your best handwriting to copy the sentence below.

What kind of fish lives in the ocean and goes perfectly with peanut butter? Jellyfish!

© Scholastic Inc.

Use your best handwriting to copy the words.

were

nobody

say

Extra Wacky! More people in the world own cellphones than toothbrushes.

Use your best handwriting to copy the sentence below.

When telephones were first invented, nobody was sure how to answer them. So people would just say, "Ahoy!"

AHOY!

Use your best handwriting to copy the words.

birds

fly

winter

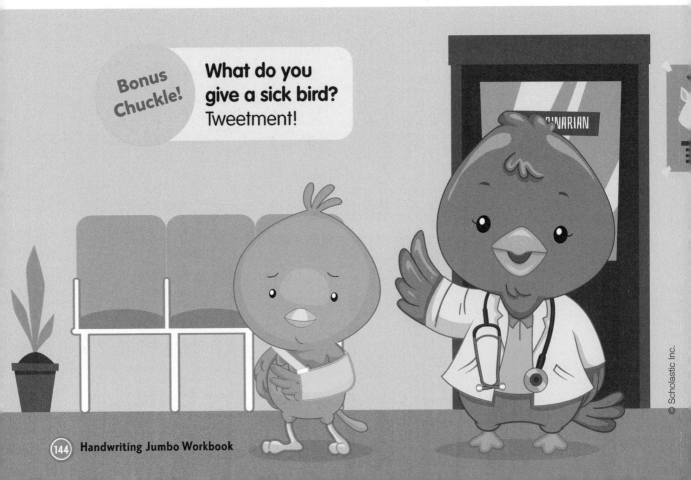

Bonus Chuckle!

What do you give a sick bird? Tweetment!

Use your best handwriting to copy the sentence below.

Why do birds always fly south in the winter? Because it is way too far for them to walk!

Use your best handwriting to copy the words.

new

year

forgot

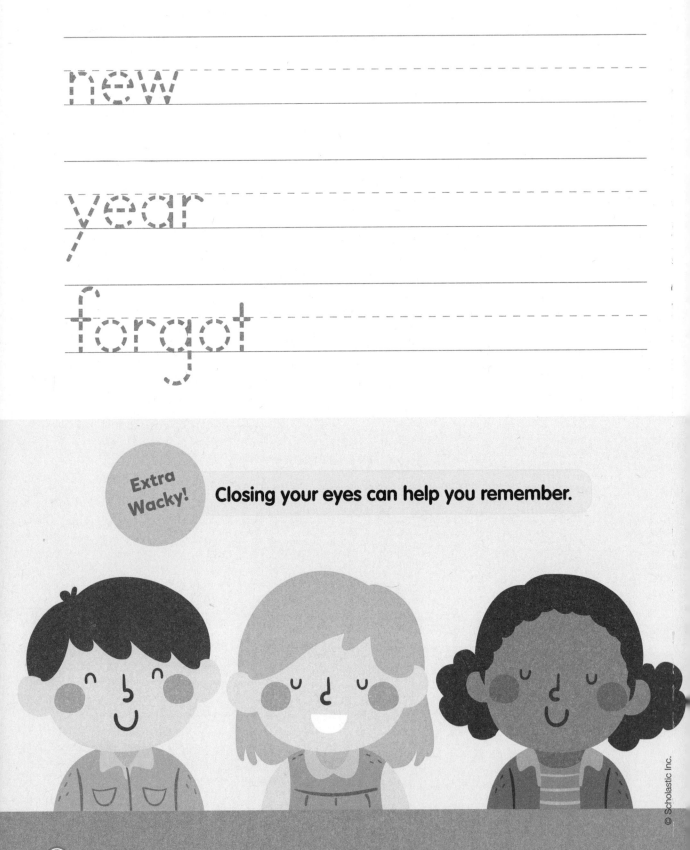

Extra Wacky! **Closing your eyes can help you remember.**

Use your best handwriting to copy the sentence below.

Millions and millions of new trees grow each year from nuts that squirrels forgot about and left buried in the ground.

Trace and write.

salty

sweet

sour

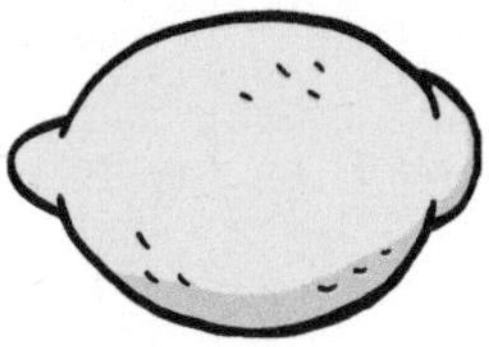

spicy

hot

cold

Draw a picture of something you love that is salty, sweet, sour, spicy, hot, or cold. Write about it using a describing word.

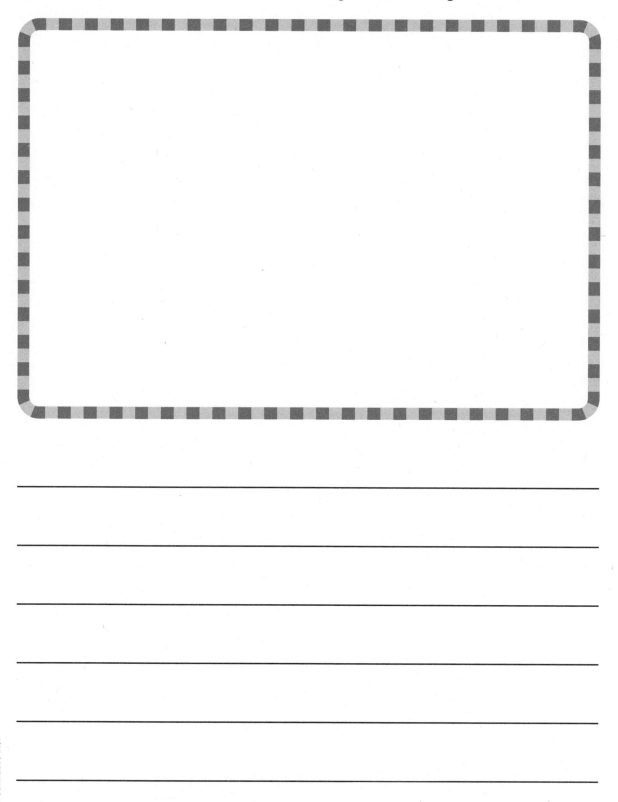

Use your best handwriting to copy the words.

Tip:
Try to make
all of your
letters stand
up straight.

bear

cross

skunk

Bonus Chuckle!

What is black and white and goes round and round?
A skunk stuck in a revolving door!

© Scholastic Inc.

Use your best handwriting to copy the sentence below.

What do you get when you cross a teddy bear with a skunk? Winnie the Pew!

Use your best handwriting to copy the words.

old

right

left

Extra Wacky! People take about 3,000 steps a day.

Use your best handwriting to copy the sentence below.

In the old days, a pair of shoes didn't have a right and left. Either foot went inside either shoe. Ouch! Ouch!

Use your best handwriting to copy the words.

pony

say

horse

Bonus Chuckle!

Where do sick ponies go?
The horse-pital!

HORSE-PITAL

© Scholastic Inc.

Use your best handwriting to copy the sentence below.

What did the pony say when he had a sore throat? "Excuse me, I am a little horse."

Use your best handwriting to copy the words.

four

sister

brother

Extra Wacky!

Babies smile 400 times a day.

Use your best handwriting to copy the sentence below.

Do you have a younger brother or sister? A child who is four years old asks about 437 questions each day.

Trace and write.

big

small

tall

pretty

soft

hard

Draw a picture of something you like that is big, small, tall, pretty, soft, or hard. Write about it using a describing word.

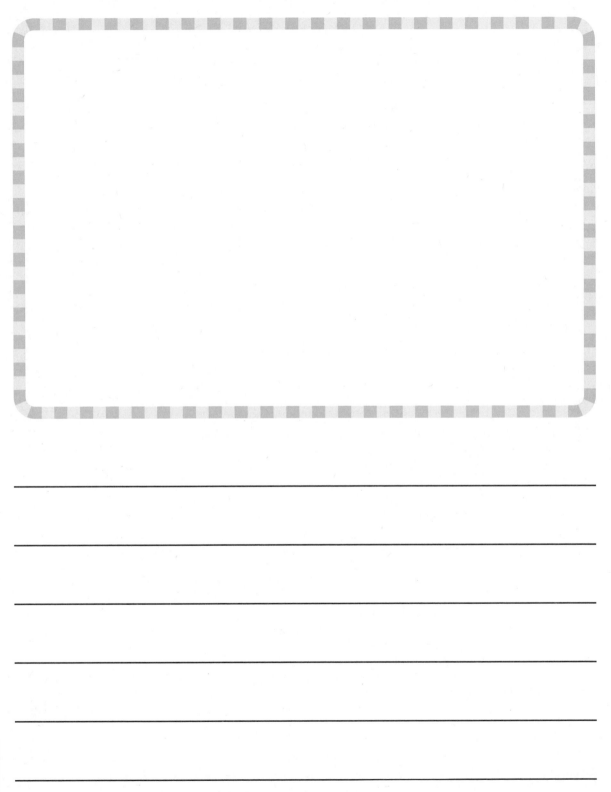

Use your best handwriting to copy the words.

Tip: If you are coming to the end of the line, begin the next word on the following line.

sharks

swim

them

Bonus Chuckle!

What happened when the shark swallowed a bunch of keys? He got lockjaw!

Use your best handwriting to copy the sentence below.

Why do sharks swim only in saltwater? Because pepper makes them sneeze!

Use your best handwriting to copy the words.

well

old

using

Extra Wacky! **Hummingbird eggs are as small as jellybeans.**

Use your best handwriting to copy the sentence below.

Brush well and enjoy your minty toothpaste. In the old days, people cleaned their teeth using ground-up eggshells.

Use your best handwriting to copy the words.

is

drink

alligator

Bonus Chuckle!

What is an alligator always wearing?
Alligator shoes!

Use your best handwriting to copy the sentence below.

What is an alligator's very favorite thing to drink? Gatorade, of course!

Use your best handwriting to copy the words.

the

mouse

made

Extra Wacky! Mickey Mouse was first drawn in 1928.

Use your best handwriting to copy the sentence below.

The computer mouse was invented in the year 1964. The very first one was made out of wood.

spring summer fall winter

Trace and write.

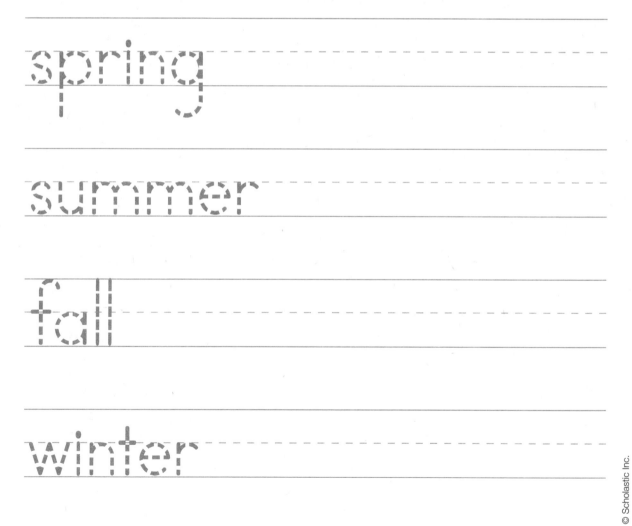

spring

summer

fall

winter

What is your favorite season? Draw a picture. Then, write about it.

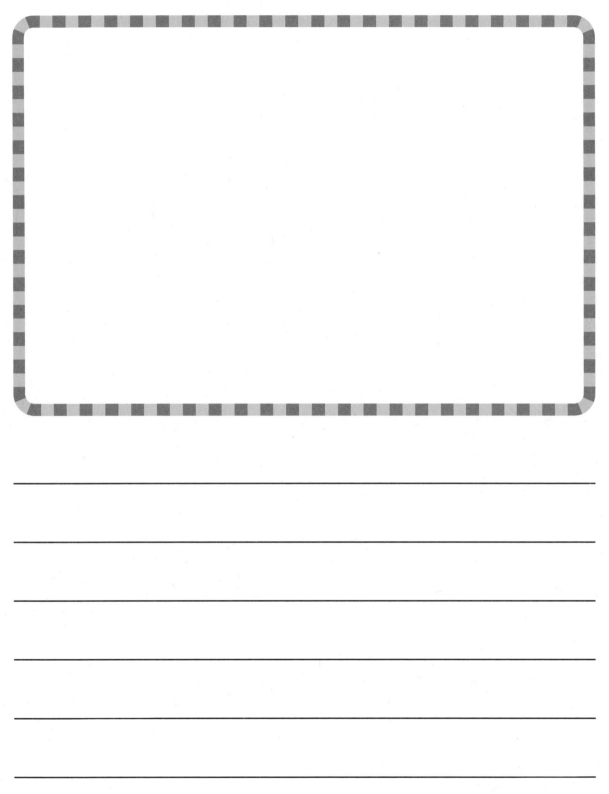

Use your best handwriting to copy the words.

Bonus Chuckle!

What do zebras have in common with old movies?
They only come in black and white!

© Scholastic Inc.

Use your best handwriting to copy the sentence below.

What is black and white and red all over? A very embarassed zebra!

Use your best handwriting to copy the words.

keep

cap

famous

Extra Wacky! The first refrigerators were more expensive than the first cars.

Use your best handwriting to copy the sentence below.

Babe Ruth, the famous baseball player, would keep a chilled cabbage leaf under his cap to stay cool. Batter up!

Use your best handwriting to copy the words.

Tip:
You can use a finger to practice writing on your friend's back.

say

parrot

duck

Bonus Chuckle!

What time does a duck wake up?
The quack of dawn!

© Scholastic Inc.

Use your best handwriting to copy the sentence below.

What did the parrot
say when he fell in love
with the duck?
"Polly want a quacker!"

Use your best handwriting to copy the words.

can

able

rhyme

Extra Wacky! **The color pink can calm you down.**

Use your best handwriting to copy the sentence below.

You can try and try and try, but you won't be able to find any words that rhyme with orange, purple, or silver.

I LIKE ORANGE AND I LIKE ???

musician nurse doctor lawyer artist teacher

writer veterinarian chef astronaut

Write the career names on the lines below.

What do you want to be when you are older? Draw a picture.
Then, write about it.

Use your best handwriting to copy the words.

Tip:
You can practice writing your letters with finger paints.

cows

field

night

Bonus Chuckle!

Why did the cow cross the road?
To get to the udder side!

Use your best handwriting to copy the sentence below.

Why were Farmer Brown's cows never in the field on a Saturday evening? That was moo-vie night!

Use your best handwriting to copy the words.

have

call

different

Extra Wacky! Some parrots can learn more than 1,000 words.

Use your best handwriting to copy the sentence below.

Dolphins have special names for one another. They use different whistles to call to their friends in the ocean.

Use your best handwriting to copy the words.

Tip: Drawing circles, squares, and triangles will help you write better letters.

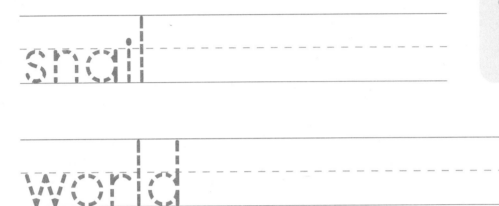

snail

world

house

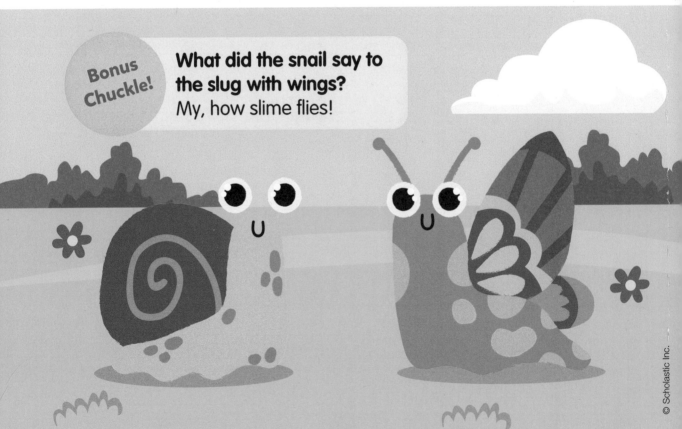

Bonus Chuckle!

What did the snail say to the slug with wings?
My, how slime flies!

Use your best handwriting to copy the sentence below.

Why is a snail the strongest animal in the world? No other creature can carry a whole house on its back!

Use your best handwriting to copy the words.

Your

better

it

Extra Wacky!   Right after a big meal, you hear less well.

Use your best handwriting to copy the sentence below.

Your sense of smell keeps getting better each year until age 8. After that, it stays the same for many years.

mother father sister brother
grandmother grandfather
cousin aunt uncle

Write the names of people in a family on the lines below.

Draw a picture of your family. Then, write about your family.

Use your best handwriting to copy the words.

Tip:
Practice your handwriting a little each day.

bats

live

hang

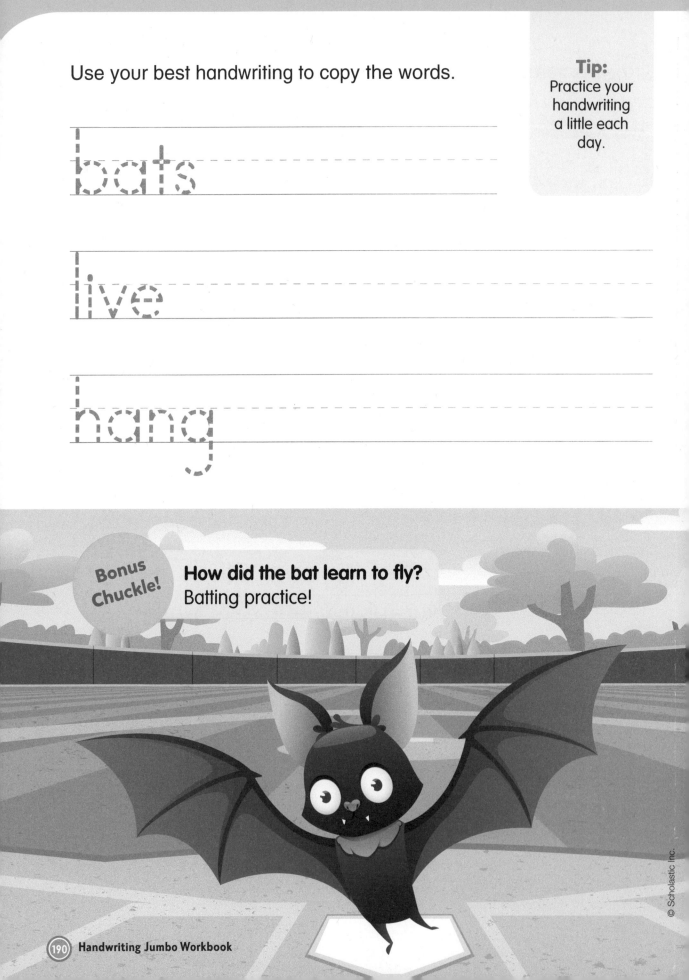

Bonus Chuckle!

How did the bat learn to fly?
Batting practice!

© Scholastic Inc.

Use your best handwriting to copy the sentence below.

Why do bats always
live in gigantic groups?
Because they love to
hang out with their friends!

Use your best handwriting to copy the words.

used

stone

glass

Extra Wacky!

Sunglasses were invented about a thousand years ago in China.

Use your best handwriting to copy the sentence below.

Before there were glasses, people used something called a reading stone. This round piece of glass made words larger.

Use your best handwriting to copy the words.

Tip:
Make sure your pencil is nice and sharp before you begin writing.

parrot

centipede

when

Bonus Chuckle!

Why was the centipede late for the party? He decided to put on his shoes!

Use your best handwriting to copy the sentence below.

What do you get when you cross a centipede with a very chatty parrot? A walkie-talkie!

TALK TALK
TALK TALK
TALK
TALK

Use your best handwriting to copy the words.

seed

the

record

Extra Wacky! **In strong wind, a dandelion seed can travel 500 miles.**

© Scholastic Inc.

Use your best handwriting to copy the sentence below.

The record for spitting a watermelon seed is 68 feet. That is the length of a yellow school bus!

Halloween

Eid al-Fitr

Cinco de Mayo

Christmas

Rosh Hashanah

Yom Kippur

Ramadan

Martin Luther King Jr. Day

Easter

Passover

Thanksgiving

Juneteenth

Eid al-Adha

Write the names of the holidays on the lines below.

© Scholastic Inc.

Draw a picture of your favorite holiday. Then, write about it.

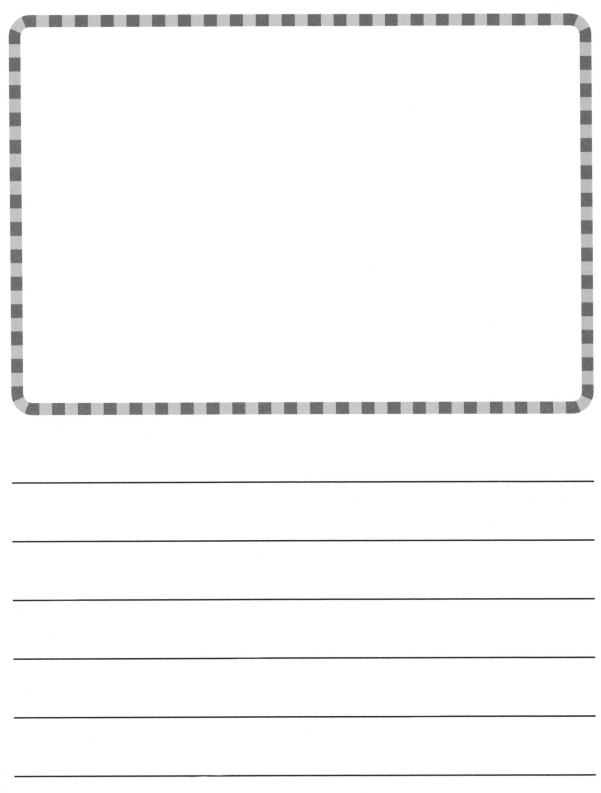

_____

_____

_____

_____

_____

Use your best handwriting to copy the words.

cross

tide

dolphin

Bonus Chuckle!

How do dolphins make a decision?
Flipper coin!

Use your best handwriting to copy the sentence below.

Why did the bottlenose dolphin cross the Atlantic Ocean? To get to the other tide!

Use your best handwriting to copy the words.

sun

huge

million

Extra Wacky! It takes eight minutes for the sun's light to travel to Earth.

© Scholastic Inc.

Use your best handwriting to copy the sentence below.

The sun is way larger than Earth. Picture the sun as a huge gumball machine. A million Earths would fit inside it!

Use your best handwriting to copy the words.

dog

hen

eggs

Bonus Chuckle!

What is the opposite of a cock-a-doodle-doo?
A cock-a-doodle-don't!

© Scholastic Inc.

Use your best handwriting to copy the sentence below.

What do you get when you cross a hen with a hound dog? Pooched eggs!

Use your best handwriting to copy the words.

can

many

even

Eating cheese can help prevent tooth decay.

Use your best handwriting to copy the sentence below.

Cheese can be made from the milk of many different animals. There is even donkey and camel cheese!

Write each question word on the lines below.

Think of a person you would like to interview. Then, write six to eight questions you would like to ask this person. Use each of these question words at least once: *who, what, when, where, why, how.*

Use your best handwriting to copy the words.

bees

always

can

Bee

Bonus Chuckle!

What's even more impressive than a talking bird?
A spelling bee!

Use your best handwriting to copy the sentence below.

Why are bees always humming? Because they can never remember all of the words!

Use your best handwriting to copy the words.

bulb

dark

good

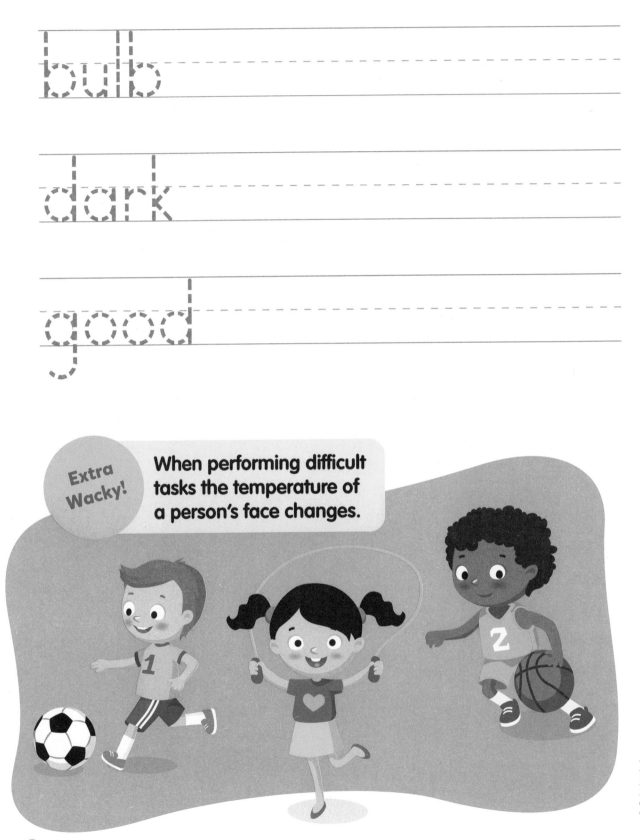

Extra Wacky!

When performing difficult tasks the temperature of a person's face changes.

Use your best handwriting to copy the sentence below.

Thomas Edison helped to make light bulbs long-lasting. That's a good thing because he was afraid of the dark!

Use your best handwriting to copy the words.

Tip:
Have a good time! Handwriting is fun.

the

he

bullfrog

Bonus Chuckle!

What happened to the frog's car?
It got toad away!

Use your best handwriting to copy the sentence below.

What happened when the bullfrog broke his leg? He became very unhoppy!

Use your best handwriting to copy the words.

ball

weighs

much

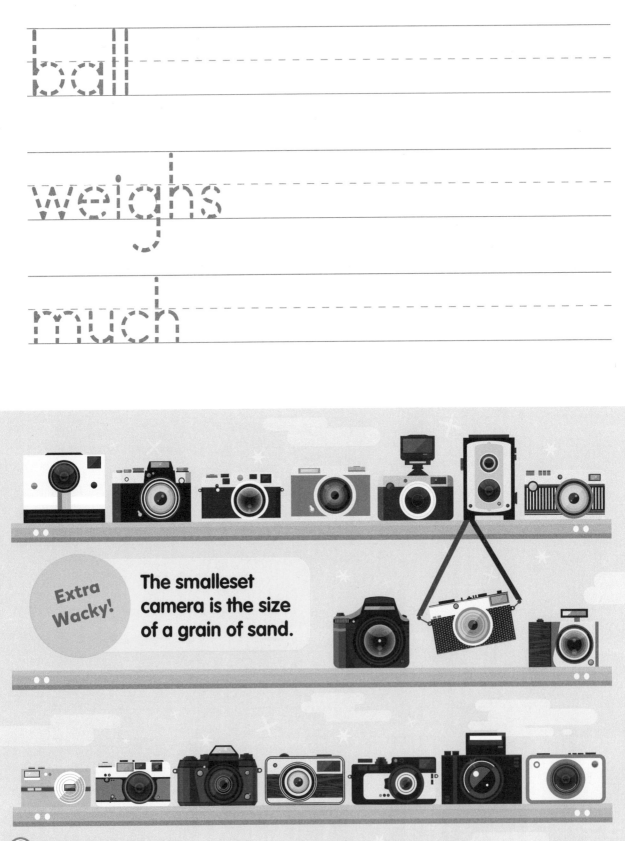

Extra Wacky! The smalleset camera is the size of a grain of sand.

Use your best handwriting to copy the sentence below.

The world's largest rubber-band ball was started in 2004. It has 700,000 rubber bands and weighs as much as an elephant!

Draw a picture of your best friend.

Draw a picture of you and your best friend together.

Read the questions below. Use them to write about your best friend.

(1) What is your best friend's name?

(2) Where did you meet your best friend?

(3) Why is this person your best friend?

(4) What do you like to do with your best friend?

_____

_____

_____

_____

_____

_____

_____

_____

Use your best handwriting to copy the words.

Tip:
Begin letters from the top, not the bottom.

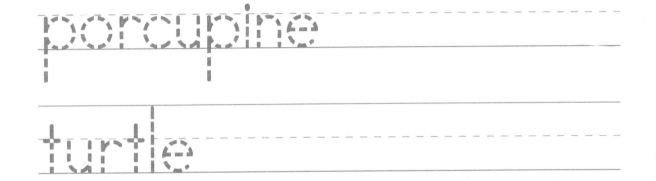

do

porcupine

turtle

Bonus Chuckle!

How do turtles communicate with other turtles?
Shell phones!

© Scholastic Inc.

Use your best handwriting to copy the sentence below.

What do you get when you cross a porcupine with a turtle? A real slowpoke!

Use your best handwriting to copy the words.

fish

and

amazing

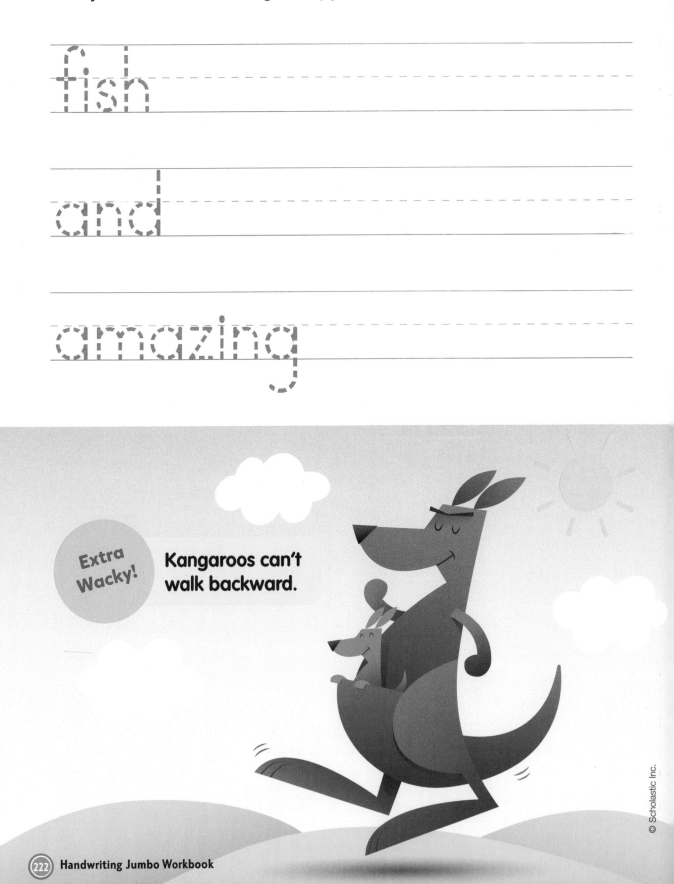

Extra Wacky!   **Kangaroos can't walk backward.**

Use your best handwriting to copy the sentence below.

Eels are amazing! These long, skinny fish have special skills, like tying their bodies in knots and swimming backward.

Use your best handwriting to copy the words.

Tip:
Pull the pencil toward the middle of your body when you write.

to

was

butterfly

BUTTER

Bonus Chuckle!

Why did the little boy throw butter out the window?
He wanted to see the butter fly!

Use your best handwriting to copy the sentence below.

Why wasn't the butterfly invited to the dance? Because the dance was a moth-ball!

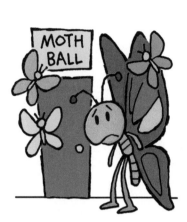

Use your best handwriting to copy the words.

your

one

trick

Extra Wacky! You blink about 25,000 times a day!

Use your best handwriting to copy the sentence below.

Can you touch your tongue to your nose? Give it a try! Only about one in ten people can do this nifty trick.

What is your favorite place? Draw a picture.

Read the questions below. Use them to write about your favorite place.

1. Where is your favorite place?
2. When do you go to your favorite place?
3. What do you do at your favorite place?
4. Why do you like this place so much?

_____

_____

_____

_____

_____

_____

_____

_____

Use your best handwriting to copy the words.

rhino

phone

two

Bonus Chuckle!

What should you do if you see a blue rhino?
Cheer it up!

© Scholastic Inc.

Use your best handwriting to copy the sentence below.

What is harder than getting a rhino into a phone booth? Getting two rhinos into a phone booth!

Use your best handwriting to copy the words.

was

president

any

Extra Wacky!

George Washington loved ice cream.

ICE CREAM

Use your best handwriting to copy the sentence below.

When John Tyler was president, the
White House was crowded.
He had 15 children, more
than any other president.

GOODNIGHT GOODNIGHT
GOODNIGHT GOODNIGHT
GOODNIGHT GOODNIGHT
GOODNIGHT GOODNIGHT

Use your best handwriting to copy the words.

Tip:
All uppercase letters should touch the top and bottom lines.

girl

oil

mouse

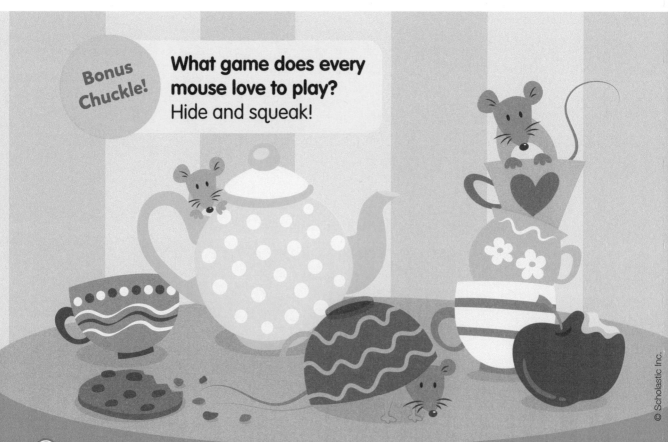

Bonus Chuckle!

What game does every mouse love to play?
Hide and squeak!

© Scholastic Inc.

Use your best handwriting to copy the sentence below.

Why did the little girl pour oil on her new pet mouse? Because it was squeaking!

Use your best handwriting to copy the words.

world

two

hours

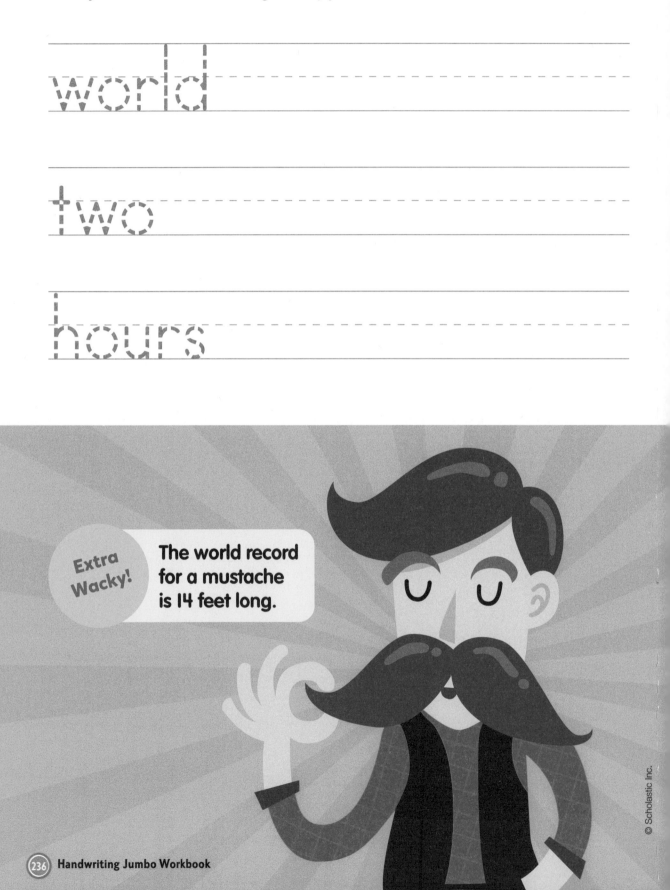

Extra Wacky! The world record for a mustache is 14 feet long.

Use your best handwriting to copy the sentence below.

The world record for longest handshake is held by two brothers. They shook hands for 42 hours and 35 minutes. Amazing!

Find and read each part of a thank-you note below.

A thank-you note is a type of letter. It has five parts: date, greeting, body, closing, and signature.

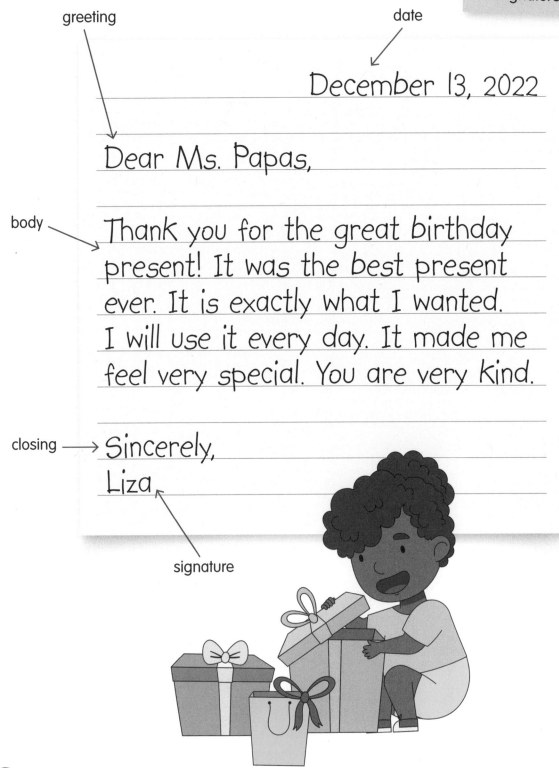

greeting

date

December 13, 2022

Dear Ms. Papas,

body

Thank you for the great birthday present! It was the best present ever. It is exactly what I wanted. I will use it every day. It made me feel very special. You are very kind.

closing → Sincerely,
Liza

signature

What are you grateful for? Draw a picture below. Then, write a thank-you note.

Dear _____,

Thank you for _____

_____

_____

Sincerely,

_____

Use your best handwriting to copy the words.

go

bite

mosquito

Bonus Chuckle!

What do you get when you cross a mosquito and a snowman?
Frostbite!

Use your best handwriting to copy the sentence below.

Why did the mosquito go to see the dentist? He wanted to improve his bite!

Use your best handwriting to copy the words.

Slow

city

tiny

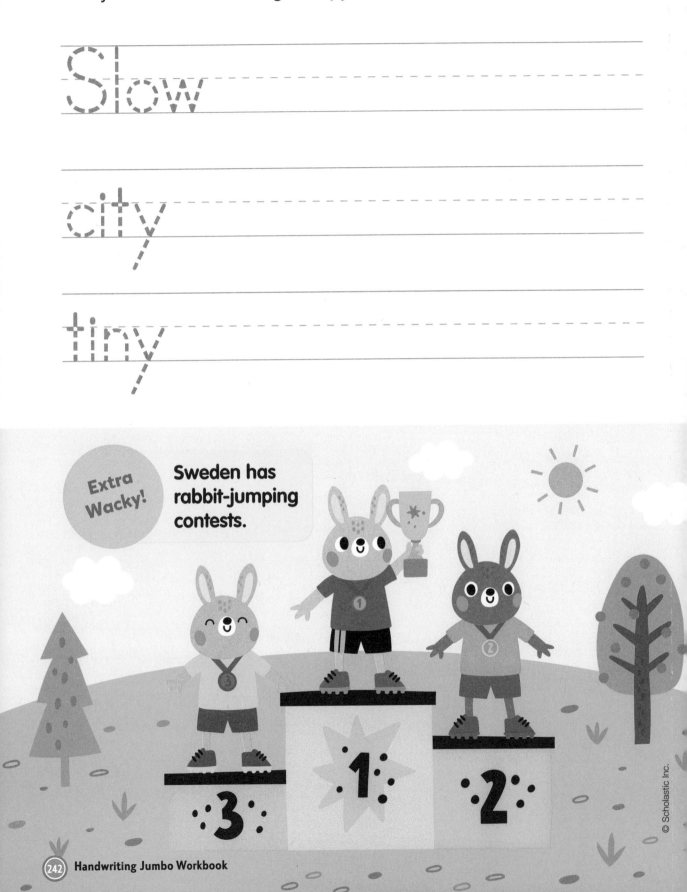

Extra Wacky! Sweden has rabbit-jumping contests.

Use your best handwriting to copy the sentence below.

On your mark. Get set. Slow! The city of Portland, Oregon, has a tiny park that is used for the sport of snail races.

Use your best handwriting to copy the words.

pig

home

school

Bonus Chuckle!

Where did the pioneer keep his pigs? In a hog cabin!

© Scholastic Inc.

Use your best handwriting to copy the sentence below.

Why did the little pig go straight home after school? He had lots of ham-work to do!

Use your best handwriting to copy the words.

days

hard

sing

Extra Wacky! Jack-o'-lanterns used to be carved out of potatoes instead of pumpkins.

Use your best handwriting to copy the sentence below.

In the old days, kids had to work hard for Halloween treats. Often, they had to dance or sing to get fruit and candy!

Write your ideas on how to do or make something. Draw a picture for each step.

A how-to paragraph tells how to do or make something. It includes a list of step-by-step instructions. A how-to guide can be about anything—for example: how to make a sandwich, brush your teeth, or play a game.

How to _____

Materials needed

_____   _____   _____

_____   _____   _____

Step 1: _____

_____

_____

Step 2: _____

_____

_____

Step 3: _____

_____

_____

© Scholastic Inc.

Write a how-to paragraph. Use the steps you outlined on page 248. Then, draw a picture of what it looks like when it is finished.

Title: _____

Written by: _____

_____

_____

_____

_____

_____

Use your best handwriting to copy the words.

Tip:
Try to make
all of your
letters stand
straight up.

get

chicken

slide

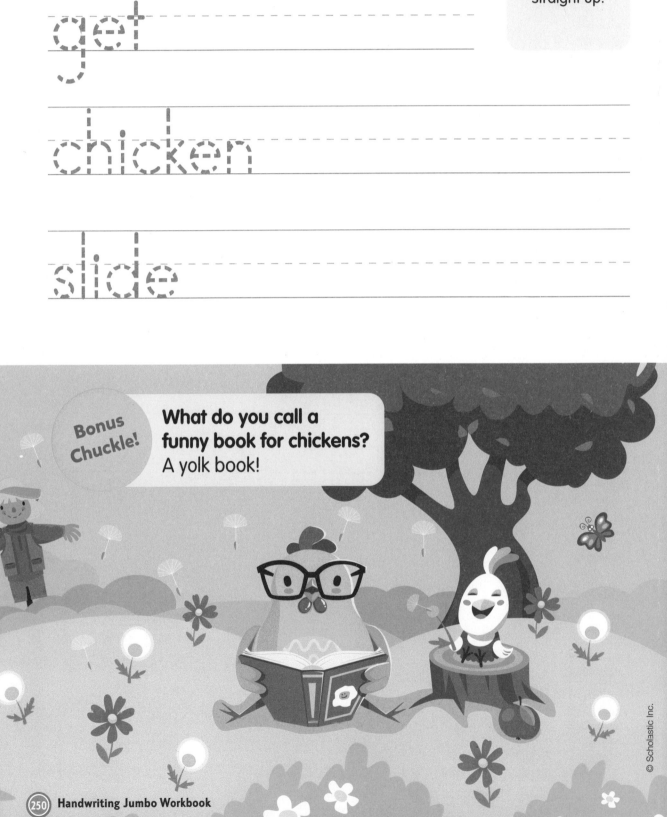

Bonus Chuckle!

What do you call a funny book for chickens?
A yolk book!

Use your best handwriting to copy the sentence below.

Why did the chicken cross the playground? He wanted to get to the other slide!

Use your best handwriting to copy the words.

more

used

kids

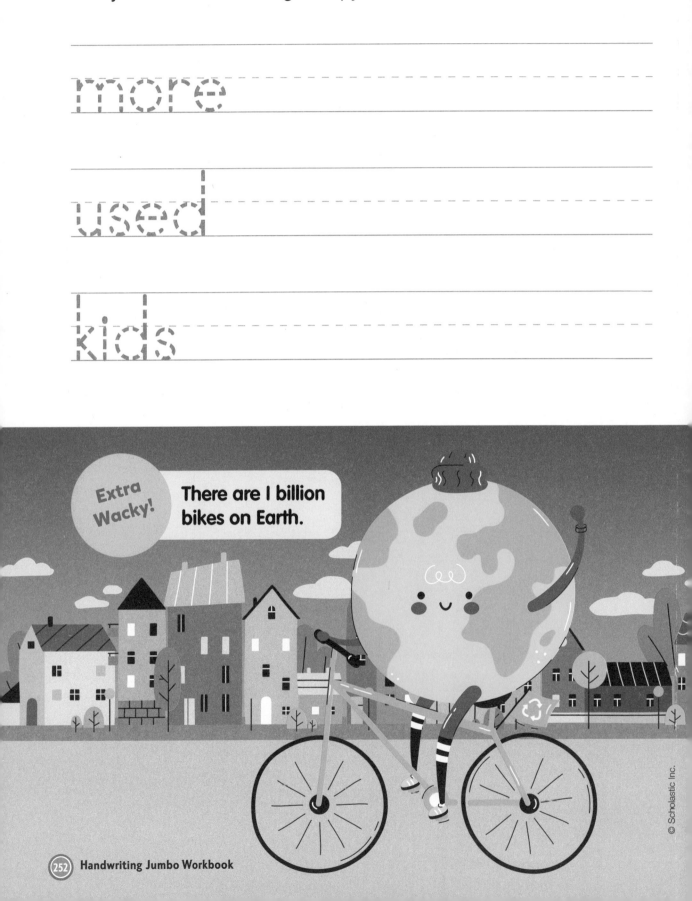

Extra Wacky!

There are 1 billion bikes on Earth.

© Scholastic Inc.

Use your best handwriting to copy the sentence below.

Tricycles were invented more than 200 years ago. The first ones were used by grown-ups rather than kids.

Use your best handwriting to copy the words.

ant

great

uncle

Bonus Chuckle!

Where do ants like to go on vacation?
Fr-ants!

Use your best handwriting to copy the sentence below.

What do you call an ant that lives with your great uncle? Your great ant, of course!

Use your best handwriting to copy the words.

of

dogs

just

Extra Wacky!

Blue whales are bigger than the biggest dinosaurs.

Use your best handwriting to copy the sentence below.

Dinosaurs were bothered by pesky fleas just like dogs are. These were giant fleas with stingers the size of needles!

SCRATCH SCRATCH

Use the spaces below to plan a book report on your favorite book.

A book report tells about a book. It includes the title and the author's name, lists important characters, tells where the story takes place, and describes the story.

Title: _____

Written by: _____

Main characters:

_____

_____

_____

The story takes place:

_____

_____

Beginning:

_____

_____

Middle:

_____

_____

End:

_____

_____

Write a book report on your favorite book.
Use your notes from page 258.

A book report uses details from the story to tell what the reader liked about the story.

_____

_____

_____

_____

_____

_____

_____

_____

Use your best handwriting to copy the words.

worm

apple

half

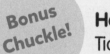
Bonus Chuckle!

How can you tell which end of a worm is which?
Tickle both ends and see which one laughs!

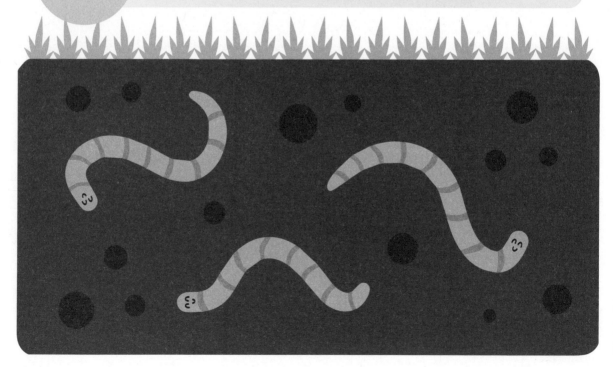

Use your best handwriting to copy the sentence below.

What is the only thing worse than finding a worm in your apple? Finding half a worm in your apple!

Use your best handwriting to copy the words.

are

planets

rains

Extra Wacky!

Venus is covered in volcanoes.

Use your best handwriting to copy the sentence below.

Are there storms in outer space?
Some scientists think it rains
diamonds on the planets
Saturn and Jupiter!

Use your best handwriting to copy the words.

wide

whole

rabbit

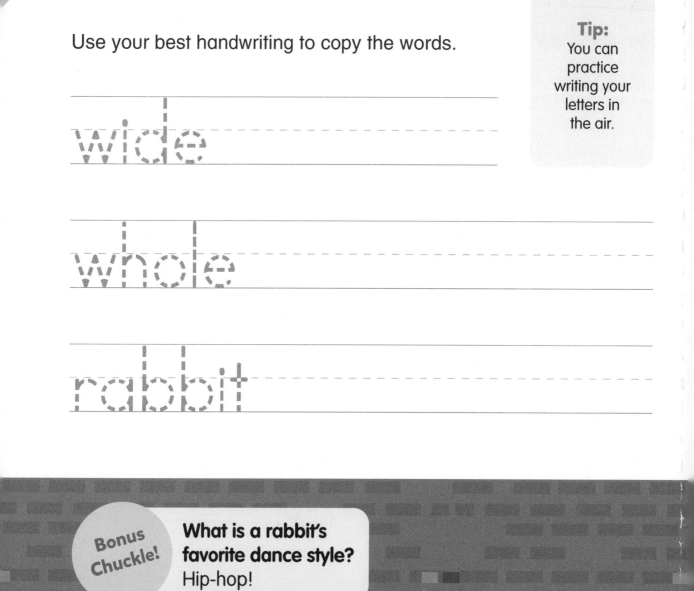

Bonus Chuckle!

What is a rabbit's favorite dance style?
Hip-hop!

Use your best handwriting to copy the sentence below.

Who is the strongest rabbit in the whole wide world? Hare-cules!

Use your best handwriting to copy the words.

back

what

like

Extra Wacky! Strawberries are not berries. They are flowers likes roses.

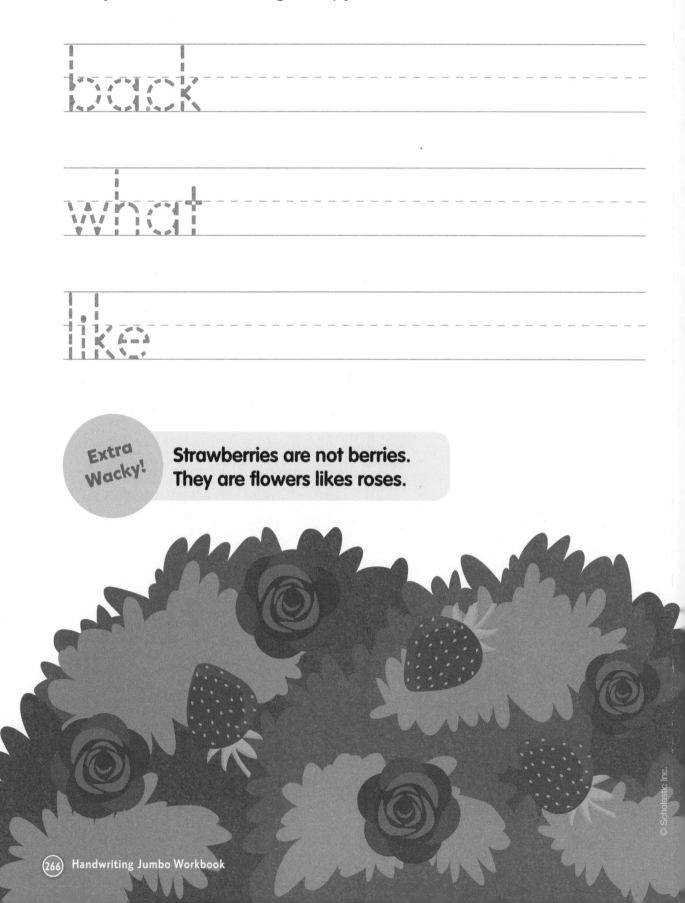

Use your best handwriting to copy the sentence below.

Drop a super ball and it will bounce back up. Guess what? Ripe cranberries also bounce like balls. Give it a try!

Write four words that describe a good role model.

A role model is someone that others look up to.

① _____

② _____

③ _____

④ _____

Write two things a good role model might do.

① _____

② _____

Write two things a good role model might say.

Write about your role model. Then, draw a picture of you with your role model.

Title: _____

Written by: _____

_____

_____

_____

_____

_____

Use your best handwriting to copy the words.

fly

between

bird

Bonus Chuckle!

Why did the fly fly?
Because the spider spied'er!

Use your best handwriting to copy the sentence below.

What is the difference between a fly and a bird? A bird can fly but a fly cannot bird!

Use your best handwriting to copy the words.

long

around

very

Extra Wacky! Cavemen had short lives. Fifteen was an old caveman.

Use your best handwriting to copy the sentence below.

Toothpicks have been around for a long, long time. How long? The very first ones were used by cavemen.

Use your best handwriting to copy the words.

274

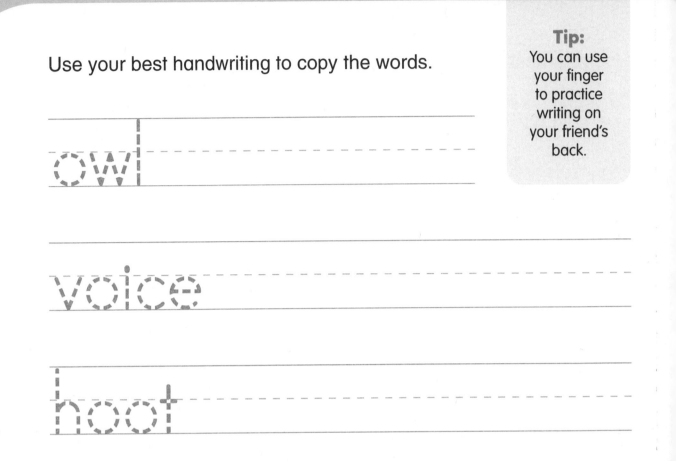

owl

voice

hoot

Bonus Chuckle!

What is green and loves to peck at trees? Woody Wood-pickle!

Use your best handwriting to copy the sentence below.

What happened when the owl lost its voice? Nothing, because it did not give a hoot!

Use your best handwriting to copy the words.

time

any

their

Extra Wacky!   A newborn giraffe can stand up after one hour.

© Scholastic Inc.

Use your best handwriting to copy the sentence below.

Elephants spend the longest time pregnant of any mammal. Female elephants carry their babies for two whole years!

Think of a topic that you know well. Then, plan your informational paragraph below.

An informational paragraph gives details about a topic. It includes a topic sentence, facts about the topic, and a closing sentence.

Topic Sentence

_____

Fact #1 ·····································

_____

_____

Fact #2 ·····································

_____

_____

Fact #3 ·····································

_____

_____

Closing Sentence ····························

_____

Write an informational paragraph. Use your notes from page 278.

Title: _____

Written by: _____

_____

_____

_____

_____

_____

_____

_____

_____

Use your best handwriting to copy the words.

not

turkey

prove

Bonus Chuckle!

What is a turkey's favorite dessert?
Peach gobbler!

Use your best handwriting to copy the sentence below.

Why did the turkey decide to skydive? He had to prove that he was not chicken!

Use your best handwriting to copy the words.

oldest

trees

years

Extra Wacky!

An alligator can live to be 100.

100

Use your best handwriting to copy the sentence below.

The oldest living things on Earth are trees. There are some ancient trees that are more than 5,000 years old.

Use your best handwriting to copy the words.

Tip: Drawing circles, squares, and triangles will help you write better letters.

joke

snakes

funny

Bonus Chuckle!

What is a snake's favorite subject in school? Hiss-story!

© Scholastic Inc.

Use your best handwriting to copy the sentence below.

What do snakes say when they hear a very funny joke?
"That was so hiss-terical!"

Use your best handwriting to copy the words.

is

days

celebrate

Extra Wacky! **January 13 is Rubber-Ducky Day.**

Use your best handwriting to copy the sentence below.

There are lots of special days
to celebrate! September 5
is Cheese Pizza Day, and
July 10 is Teddy Bear Picnic Day.

Use the spaces below to plan your own comic strip.

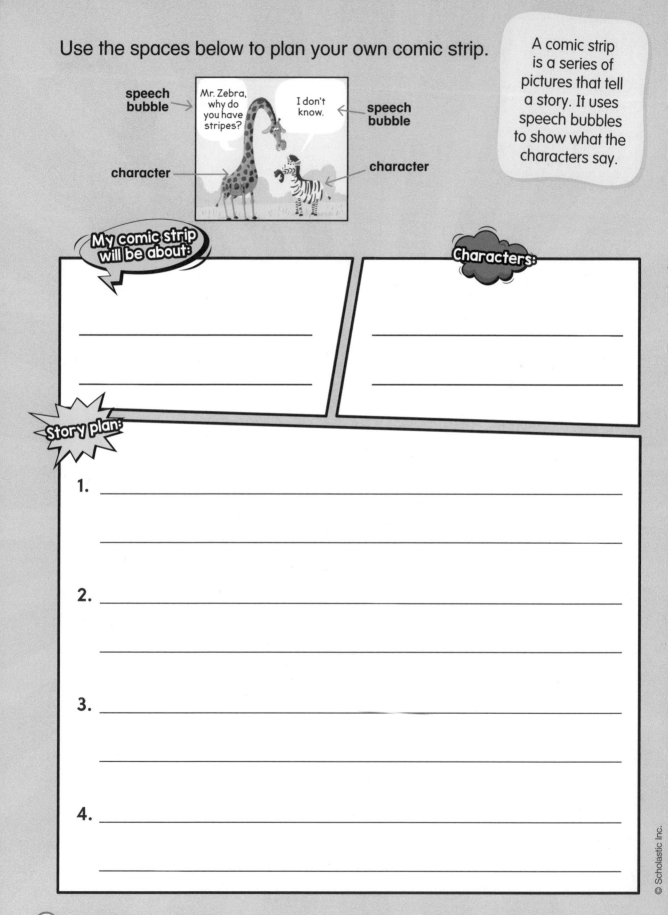

A comic strip is a series of pictures that tell a story. It uses speech bubbles to show what the characters say.

speech bubble → Mr. Zebra, why do you have stripes?

I don't know. ← speech bubble

character →

character →

My comic strip will be about:

_____

_____

Characters:

_____

_____

Story plan:

1. _____

_____

2. _____

_____

3. _____

_____

4. _____

_____

Draw and write your comic strip. Use your notes from page 288.

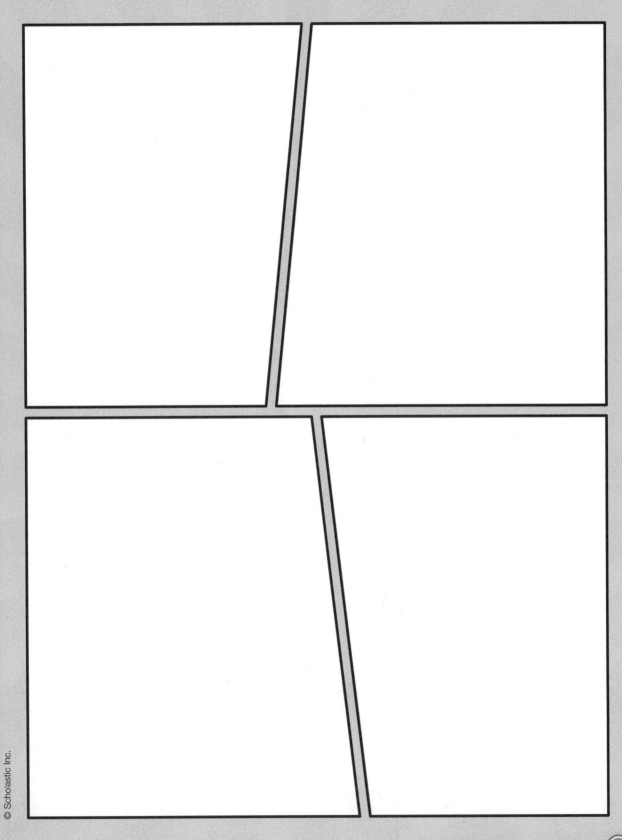

Use your best handwriting to copy the words.

in

long

leopard

Bonus Chuckle!

What is the difference between a tiger and a lion?
A tiger has the mane part missing!

Use your best handwriting to copy the sentence below.

Did you hear what happened to the leopard who stayed in the shower too long? He became spotless!

Use your best handwriting to copy the words.

was

candy

after

Extra Wacky! Cotton candy used to be called "fairy floss."

Use your best handwriting to copy the sentence below.

What favorite candy was invented in 1908? The lollipop! This sweet treat was named after a famous racehorse.

Use your best handwriting to copy the words.

for

giraffe

school

Bonus Chuckle!

What do giraffes have that no other animal has?
Baby giraffes!

Use your best handwriting to copy the sentence below.

Why was the little giraffe late for school? Because his mom got stuck in a huge giraffic jam!

HONK! HONK!

Use your best handwriting to copy the words.

may

simply

tickle

Extra Wacky!   **Very few people can wiggle their ears.**

Use your best handwriting to copy the sentence below.

You may be a little ticklish or a lot ticklish. But either way, it is simply not possible to tickle yourself.

Think of a short story of your own. Add details about your idea to the story map below.

A story has a beginning, a middle, and an end. A story also has characters and a setting. Characters are the people or animals in a story. The setting is where a story takes place.

Characters

_____

_____

Setting

_____

_____

Beginning	Middle	End
_____	_____	_____
_____	_____	_____
_____	_____	_____
_____	_____	_____
_____	_____	_____
_____	_____	_____

Write a short story. Use the characters, setting, and ideas from your story map.

Title: _____

Written by: _____

_____

_____

_____

_____

_____

_____

_____

_____

Use your best handwriting to copy the words.

to

see

kangaroo

Bonus Chuckle!

What is a kangaroo's favorite season?
Spring!

Use your best handwriting to copy the sentence below.

Why did the kangaroo hop over to see his doctor? He was feeling quite jumpy!

DR. WOMBAT

Use your best handwriting to copy the words.

sport

moon

hit

Extra Wacky!

The earth has earthquakes and the moon has moonquakes.

Use your best handwriting to copy the sentence below.

Golf is the first sport to be played on the moon. An astronaut hit a golf ball there, and it glided slowly through space.

Use your best handwriting to copy the words.

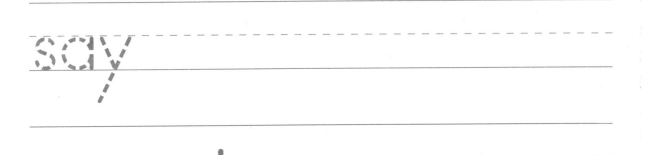

little

say

penguin

Bonus Chuckle!

What is a penguin's favorite drink?
A waddle bottle!

Use your best handwriting to copy the sentence below.

What did the ocean say
to the little penguin?
Nothing. It just waved!

Use your best handwriting to copy the words.

fins

by

only

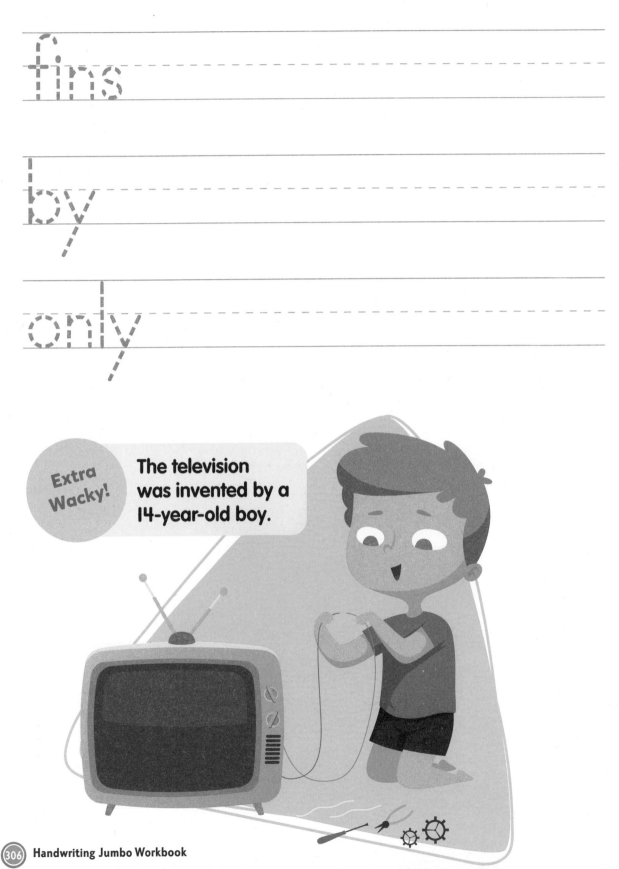

Extra Wacky!

The television was invented by a 14-year-old boy.

Use your best handwriting to copy the sentence below.

Swim fins were invented by Ben Franklin when he was only 11 years old. Ben thought swimming was great exercise!

Think up a fable of your own. Add details about your idea to the story map below.

A fable is a story that teaches a lesson. For example, a lesson might be "always believe in yourself." The main characters in a fable are usually animals.

Characters:

Setting:

Beginning:

Middle:

End:

Lesson:

Write your fable. Use the characters, setting, and ideas from your story map.

Title: _____

Written by: _____

_____

_____

_____

_____

_____

_____

_____

_____

Use your best handwriting to copy the words.

Tip:
Always try
your very
best.

did

spider

crawl

Bonus Chuckle!

Why did the spider buy a car?
He wanted to go for a spin!

© Scholastic Inc.

Use your best handwriting to copy the sentence below.

Why did the spider crawl across the computer keyboard? He wanted to make a Web site!

Use your best handwriting to copy the words.

park

looked

very

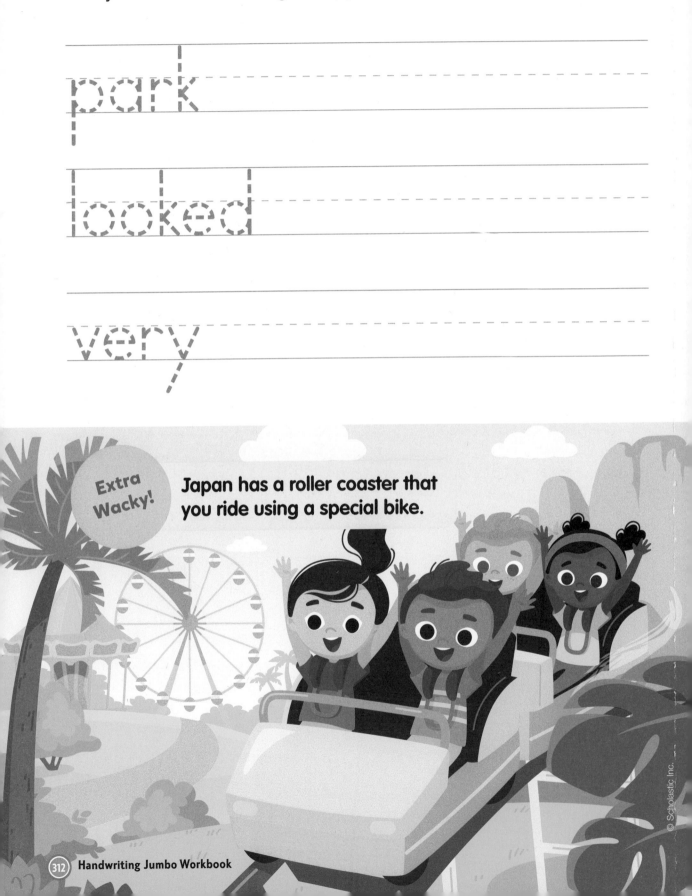

Extra Wacky!

Japan has a roller coaster that you ride using a special bike.

Use your best handwriting to copy the sentence below.

One of the first roller coasters looked like a park bench on wheels. There was no seatbelt because it moved very slowly.

Use your best handwriting to copy the words.

Tip:
Have a good time! Handwriting is fun.

rain

bear

grizzly

Bonus Chuckle!

What is a polar bear's very favorite food?
A brrr-grrr!

Use your best handwriting to copy the sentence below.

What do you call a grizzly bear that gets caught in the rain? A drizzly bear!

Use your best handwriting to copy the words.

is

number

write

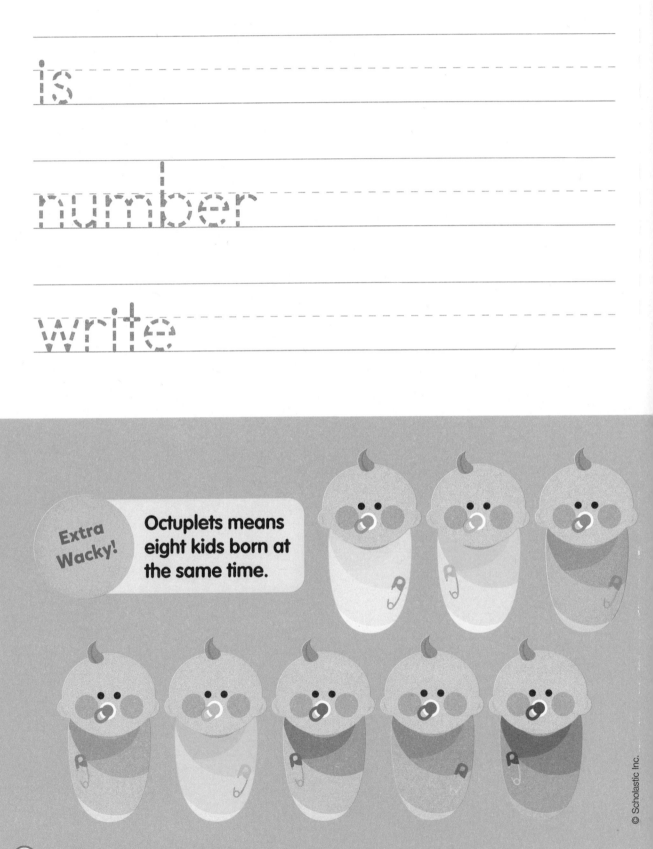

Extra Wacky! Octuplets means eight kids born at the same time.

Use your best handwriting to copy the sentence below.

Googol is a number. It's way bigger than a million. You write a googol with a 1 followed by one hundred zeros.

Write an autobiography about yourself.
Share it with a friend.

An autobiography is a story about a person's life, written by that person.

You're a SUPERSTAR!

has completed the

SCHOLASTIC HANDWRITING JUMBO WORKBOOK!

name

Congratulations!

date